BERNAS ESTOCADAS

Grandmaster
WILLIAM BERNAS

With
PAOLO PAGALING
& ROBERT J. PARKES

VOLUME 1: ABESEDARIO
Fundamentals of the Bernas Way of Filipino Martial Arts

Published by ESKRIMA MEDIA
Newcastle, Australia

Copyright © 2022 William Bernas, Paolo Pagaling & Robert J. Parkes

ALL RIGHTS RESERVED

No part of this publication may be reproduced or transmitted in any form or by any means, electronic, mechanical or photographic, by recording or any information storage or retrieval system or method now known or to be invented or adapted, without prior permission obtained in writing from the publisher, except where brief passages are used in a review written by a reviewer for inclusion in a journal, magazine, newspaper, blog or broadcast.

DISCLAIMER

Please note that the publisher and authors of this instructional book are NOT RESPONSIBLE in any manner whatsoever for any injury that may result from practicing the techniques and/or following the instruction given within. martial arts training can be dangerous - both to you and to others. If you are in doubt as to how to proceed or whether your practice is safe, consult with a qualified martial arts instructor before beginning. Since the physical activities described herein may be too strenuous in nature for some readers, it is also essential that a physician be consulted prior to the commencement of training.

ACKNOWLEDGEMENT

The authors would like to thank Manunúdlò Chris Baird who proof read drafts of the chapters as we were developing them, providing valuable feedback that improved the final version of this text.

FIRST PUBLISHED JANUARY 2022

Designed and Edited by Robert J. Parkes
Original Photography by Paolo Pagaling
Demonstrations by William Bernas & Paolo Pagaling

PRINT ISBN 978-0-6453625-0-3
E-BOOK ISBN 978-0-6453625-1-0

For further information:
www.estocadas.net/eskrimamedia

INTRODUCTION

The Filipino Martial Arts (FMA) are combative traditions from Luzon and the Visayas, the Christianised northern and middle regions of the Philippine archipelago, that for more than three hundred years formed part of the colonies of Spain. The most popular term in the Philippines for FMA is arguably *Arnis*, a local pronunciation of the Spanish *Arnés*, that originally referred to the armour of a *caballero* (a horse-mounted warrior or knight). Remembering that knights were the medieval cavalry, the related term in English is "harness" that once referred to the "war-trappings" of the knight's horse. In Spanish, *Arnés* also came to be used to describe "arms" or weapons of warfare as well. Given that the stick used in the Filipino Martial Arts is often colloquially referred to as an *Arnis*, it is likely that the term references practitioners' skill in using their stick as both their sword and (only) armour. In the Visayas, the region where Bernas Estocadas is from, the more common term for FMA is *Eskrima*, the local pronunciation of *Esgrima*, the Spanish word for "fencing" (which evolved from the word "defence"), the Latinate equivalent of the English word "skirmish" which originally meant something like "to protect or defend" instead of its contemporary association with a disorganised and unpremeditated rumble. Certainly, to be an Eskrimador in the Visayas, is to be a person respected for their capacity to use both stick and blade with the skill of a swordsman. Historically, many other terms have also been used including *Estocada* (also spelt *Estokada)*, another term for fencing or fighting, that originally referenced a particular type of Spanish sword.

Much work still needs to be done to seperate mythology from history when trying to determine the origins of the Filipino Martial Arts. What we do know with certainty, is that Filipinos in their hundreds served in Spanish naval militia during the colonial period, defending the northern and central islands against pirate activity from the Muslim regions to the south. It is not hard to imagine these Filipino sailors with their *Bólo* as the perfect naval cutlass, a working blade that could cut rope and wood, but also work as a sword in combat. It is certainly acknowledged that by 1763, Filipinos working on Spanish ships in the Gulf of Mexico, as part of the Manila Galleon Trade (1565-1815) that operated between the ports of Manila (in the Philippines) and Acapulco (in what was then known as New Spain), were deserting their posts and starting to settle in areas like the marshlands of Louisiana, where it was hard for the Spanish to find them. Many of these "Manilamen", as they had become known, were recruited by the French-born privateer Jean Lafitte, who operated a smuggling operation out of Barataria Bay, that came to an abrupt halt when a United States naval force invaded in 1814. In exchange for a legal pardon, Jean Lafitte and his fleet assisted General Andrew Jackson during the Battle of New Orleans (1815), a late skirmish in the War of 1812. Manilamen played an important role in the battle, helping the Americans to gain their rapid victory against their British opponents. It is also known that during the Philippine Revolution of the late 1890s, revolutionaries used their *Talíbong, Ginúnting, Pinúti,* and *Bólo* against the Spaniards; and would see action in New Guinea and the Philippines during WWII as "Bolomen", serving as members of the 1st Filipino Regiment known commonly as the Bolo Battalion. Many famous Eskrima grandmasters are known to have seen combat action during this time.

The documented modern history of what we know as the Filipino Martial Arts today, arguably begins when the Cañete and Saavedra families together formed the famous Labangon Fencing Club in the early 1920s. When internal difficulties lead to its dissolution in 1931, Eulogio Cañete, Lorenzo Saavedra, and Teodoro Saavedra were quick to form what would become the famous Doce Pares club. It was in this inter-war period, where Eskrima obviously starts to move from its family or *Barangáy* based informal transmission (which of course has never completely disappeared from some parts of the Philippines), to a more structured approach to training that we recognise has evolved into the many systems, and national sport, we see today.

BERNAS ESTOCADAS

Bernas Estocadas is a comprehensive system of Filipino Martial Arts that was developed by Grandmaster William Bernas. The system draws on several styles of Eskrima from the northern part of Negros Occidental, the region of the Philippines where he grew up. As a point of reference, the Presas brothers who famously developed Modern Arnis, were from the southern part of the Negros Occidental region. The island of Negros, given its name by the Spanish because of its dark-skinned inhabitants, is less than 100 kms (just under 60 miles) from the island of Cebu, the original home of the famous Doce Pares club and the Labangon Fencing Club that had preceded it. Both Negros and Cebu are part of the Visayan region, a hotbed of many styles and systems of Eskrima.

THE EARLY WEDO INFLUENCE

One of the most important influences on Bernas Estocadas derives from when Grandmaster Bernas was only young. He was born in Escalante, and grew up in the household of his maternal Grandfather, Ciriaco Canillo. As a *Bastonero* (stick fighter), Ciriaco Canillo was seldom without his favourite *Olisi*, a walking stick of about 36 inches in length, with a curved protuberance at one end that could be used to rest your hand on. As a man who liked to drink, he would often go off in search of coconut wine, and after he had felt the influence of his wine, it was not uncommon for him to look for a sparring partner. Frequently, it was Ciriaco's grandson, the young GM Bernas, that would be his recruit.

In the beginning the sparring started out with some boxing, but as GM Bernas got a little older, Ciriaco would encourage his grandson to find a stick so they could stick-spar. The exhanges were more like play than training. However, over time his grandfather would make suggestions about how to defend, or how to strike. It was all very informal, and rather random. There was *Kinaádman* "old knowledge" or "wisdom" shared, but very little structure to the teaching.

Although he didn't know it at the time, this was GM Bernas' initial exposure to *Wedo* (from the Spanish *Oido*, meaning "hearing", and referencing someone with skill not learnt through formal instruction). What he learnt during his *Wedo* experiences would have a permanent impact on GM Bernas, and were just about to continue with his Uncle.

When he was about 10 years old, GM Bernas also started learning from his Uncle, Manoy Alfon Brinquiz. His Uncle was also skilled in the *Olisi*, and he would typically visit him on Sundays to learn what they simply called *Bastón* or *Eskrima*. There was no reference to styles or systems. Once again he would experience the *Wedo* form of informal or loose instruction. The most structured it would get would be encouragement to combine a certain set of strikes, such as an upward diagonal forehand with a downward diagonal backhand, where one strike could be used to knock the opponent's weapon away and the other to execute an immediate follow up counter. This kind of "to and fro" principle would be a strong influence on GM Bernas in the development of his system. Manoy Alfon also introduced him to the blade, specifically the *Talíbong* and *Ginúnting*. Whenever they trained in *Lab-ánay* (from the word *Labô* meaning to slash with an edged weapon), their swords would be dulled to serve as safer training instruments. Spiritual matters were also never far from *Bastón* practice, as Manoy Alfon was quiet famous in the *Barangáy* as a fighter who could not be hurt due to the power of his *Antíng-Antíng*. When he would eventually succumb to a gangrenous foot, it was believed by the family and those in the village, that Manoy Alfon had been the victim of some form of black magic curse from a local rival.

THE INFLUENCE OF THE NAVALES SYSTEM

In 1982, while GM Bernas was in college studying to be a graphic artist, his girlfriend at the time had an uncle who was a member of a *Barangáy* police unit that happened to be learning *Arnis* from Grandmaster Hortencio Navales. When GM Bernas found out that they were training at the Spanish house her uncle was renting, he asked if he could join, petitioning with the fact that he already had some experience in stick-fighting. The villa wasn't big, but had a very spacious second floor room in which the group would meet with GM Navales for instruction. Because GM Bernas was the boyfriend of the niece of the man whose house he was using as a training space, GM Navales allowed GM Bernas to join the group. He wasn't really ever a formal member of the group, but was allowed to engage in the training. It was here that GM Bernas was exposed for the first time to a systematic 12-Strike numbering system that would start him thinking about how he would arrange his own striking techniques. The training would take place once a week, and he continued until he dropped out of college in 1983, and sought work in Cebu.

GM Hortencio "Horten" Navales was originally assistant to his brother who was the initial teacher of their system. As far as anyone knows in Bacolod, his brother learned his *Arnis* from two well known *Bastóneros* in Negros, namely Juan Lawan and Mang Karpo, and also from an unknown *Arnisador* from the neighbouring island of Panay. When his brother died, he took over and taught his brother's compilation of the arts, which he openly taught at the then Navales Arnis Clinic. GM Navales' style of *Arnis* is known in Bacolod as *Pekiti Tirsia* which shouldn't be confused with the more popular Pekiti Tirsia Kali, and was simply a reference to it being "Close Quarters" fighting.

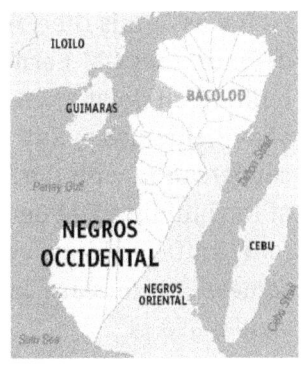

Map of Negros Occidental showing the location of Bacolod

Original Colour Image Created by
Mike Gonzalez
28 November 2005
Distributed under license:
CC BY-SA 3.0

Once in Cebu, GM Bernas made a friend who studied Karate, who also happened to be a practitioner of the Doce Pares system. Whenever they met they would practice Karate, but because GM Bernas had a background in stick-fighting and would share what he had learnt with his friend, his friend in-turn started to share what he knew of the Doce Pares system. Up until this time, GM Bernas had never seen any authentic Doce Pares, but its fame as "stick-fighting" had spread to many places, including his home city of Escalante, where the term Doce Pares had become synonymous for the locals with any form of stick-fighting. Even in Cebu today, where many systems of *Eskrima* originated as we have already noted, if you ask a Taxi driver "Do you know what Eskrima is?" you are likely to get a puzzled look. But if you ask "Do you know what Doce Pares is?" you will immediately get an excited answer of "Ah yes, stick-fighting!"

In 1985 GM Bernas returned to Bacolod. It was at this time that he had an encounter with four thugs, who he initially fought off with his bare hands. Later, the four men returned with knives to confront him again. At this point, out-numbered and without a weapon of his own, and with little sense about how to handle multiple opponents armed with knives, he withdrew and escaped. This stimulated him to seek out instruction from someone who could teach him knife defence, and motivated him to ensure his training always considered multiple opponents.

It was at this time, while seeking to find a martial art that teaches knife defence, that GM Bernas chanced upon the entrance to the old DBP Bank building in downtown Bacolod, where he recognised the name of Navales above the door. Shy to enter the building, GM Bernas struck up a conversation with the *Sorbetero* (Ice Cream vendor) who was out the front of the building. GM Bernas told the *Sorbetero* about his encounter with the four knife-wielding assailants, and explained that he was looking for somewhere to learn knife defence. He was told that he had come to the right place.

This turned out to be his first meeting with Romeo Postrano, who had trained for more than 15 years under the tutelage of Grandmaster Navales, and happened at the time to be the old Grandmaster's top student (who would later become the Grandmaster of his own system). Upon enrolling in the Navales Arnis Clinic, GM Navales assigned GM Postrano, to teach GM Bernas, and they became good friends and "kumpadre".

As time went on, GM Bernas found out that GM Postrano was also from Escalante, and that he had also learned a unique style similar to that taught to GM Bernas by his Uncle and Grandfather. It was through his interactions with GM Postrano that GM Bernas would master this style, recognising its links with his earliest FMA experiences. He would also learn that it really only went by the name *Wedo* (or *Oido*).

GM Bernas would train for three years in the Navales Arnis Clinic, and during the time he was an instructor was developing his own system, bringing together the unique *Wedo* style, together with a more structured pedagogical approach influenced and inspired by the *Arnis* he had learnt within the Navales Arnis Clinic. The result of this creative fusion is the Bernas Estocadas system, that draws on the best of the old ways, with the strength of the new.

In this volume, the core of the Bernas Estocadas system is introduced, that consists of a series of *12 Opensa* (Strikes) and *12 Depensa* (Blocks), always taught synchronised with footwork, and with attention to the movement of the *Ngangáng Buáya* (crocodile mouth), the name given in the system to the "alive hand". The main focus is on the *Solo Bastón* (single stick), but applications with the *Talíbong* (sword) are demonstrated in the final chapter that explains and demonstrates the first three levels of the core partner *Opensa-Depensa* (attack-defence) application drill. We hope you enjoy the book and we look forward to sharing more of the system with you in future volumes.

TABLE OF CONTENTS

1   **PAGSOLÓNDAN**   1
Fundamentals

2   **PANÍNDOG**   17
Stances

3   **PALAKÁT**   25
Footwork

4   **OPENSA**   33
12 Strikes

5   **DEPENSA**   63
12 Blocks

6   **PÁRES PÁRES**   91
Paired Strikes & Blocks

7   **DÁGWAY**   117
Forms

8   **OPENSA-DEPENSA**   173
Attack & Defence

1
PAGSOLÓNDAN
FUNDAMENTALS

PAGSOLÓNDAN

In this chapter we will explore the *Pagsolóndan* of the Bernas Estocadas system. In Ilonggo, *Pagsolóndan* refers to the rules of conduct to be followed, the standards, or guiding principles. In Bernas Estocadas, these fundamental principles form a foundation that is drawn upon repeatedly when practicing the techniques and tactics of the system, and include:

- **SALUDO** | The system's method of saluting and bowing to show respect or gratitude to your instructor or training partners.

- **PANGÚYAT** | The proper method of grasping or holding your *Bastón* (stick).

- **PREPARAR** | The fundamental ready stance of the system.

- **POSISYÓN** | The various ways in which the stick can be positioned, such as *Serrada* (Closed), *Abierta* (Open), and *Séntro* (Central); and including the important principles of *Kayâ* (supine) and *Kulob* (prone) positions of the weapon hand.

- **GARÁHE** | The manner of parking or chambering the stick.

- **PIGAR** | The technique of applying pressure with the alive or non-weapon hand, that is closely connected with the *Ngangáng Buáya* (Crocodile Mouth) technique.

SALUDO

Bernas Estocadas training begins and ends with a salute. Like most salutes, *Saludo* is a courtesy used to show respect, gratitude, and appreciation. If saluting a training partner, ensure that eye contact is maintained throughout the action.

Saludo can be practiced with or without a weapon. In the series of photographs below it is demonstrated with a single stick, in alignment with the focus of this volume. However, without a weapon the closed fist is brought up to the left side of the chest. All other aspects of the salute remain the same.

Start in a natural stance.

1

Bring your right foot together with your left foot.

2

Bring your weapon hand up to your left breast, tip of the weapon pointing upwards.

3

Bow while maintaining a forward gaze.

4

Return to the *Pahúway* resting position.

5

PANGÚYAT

Pangúyat means to "grasp" and refers to the method of holding or gripping the weapon. There are three steps to form a proper grip on the *Bastón* (stick):

1. Hold the stick in your right hand two or three fingers up from its base.
2. Grip firmly with your little, ring and middle fingers. Your index finger and thumb should be relaxed.
3. Close your thumb lightly on top of your index finger.

PREPARAR

Preparar is the fundamental "ready stance" of Bernas Estocadas. It is the equivalent of the *On-Guard* stance found in European fencing. *Preparar* is an attentive, balanced, and neutral position, from which either attack or defence can be launched at a split second's notice.

To assume *Preparar*, shift into a Back Stance where most of the weight is on the rear leg. Both hands are lifted, not too high, and not too low. The weapon is typically held in a *Séntro Serrada* (central closed) position, with the non-weapon "alive" hand sitting behind, ready to parry, push, or strike.

SERRADA POSISYÓN

Your weapon can be held in either an open, closed, or central position. We call the "closed" position *Serrada*. When the weapon is held in a *Serrada* position, your weapon arm covers or protects your body. You may place the weapon high over your rear shoulder (Fig. 1), middle at the level of your non-weapon arm elbow (Fig. 2), or low pointing toward your rear foot (Fig. 3).

1 High Serrada Position

2 Middle Serrada Position

3 Low Serrada Position

ABIERTA POSISYÓN

We call the "open" guard position *Abierta*. When the weapon is held in an *Abierta* position your body appears open, but is ready to be protected by your weapon. You may place the weapon high over the lead shoulder (Fig. 1), middle at the level of the weapon-arm elbow (Fig. 2), or low pointing to the ground in front of the lead foot (Fig. 3).

1. High Abierta Position

2. Middle Abierta Position

3. Low Abierta Position

SÉNTRO POSISYÓN

You may also position your weapon in a "central" position we call *Séntro*. To assume a *Séntro* position, the weapon may be placed entirely on an imaginary centreline bisecting your face and torso (Fig. 1). Assuming you are holding the weapon in your right hand, it may also be tilted towards the right side forming the *Séntro Abierta* (Open Central) position (Fig. 2), or tilted towards the left side forming the *Séntro Serrada* (Closed Central) position (Fig. 3).

1 Séntro Position

2 Séntro Abierta Position

3 Séntro Serrada Position

KAYÂ / KULOB

Another aspect of stick handling and positioning involves the specific position of the wrist of your weapon hand. Wrist position is very important in striking. The switching of the wrist position during the execution of a strike is like the last link in a chain, or a tiger's tail, helping to generate whip in the strike.

Kayâ

When your palm is facing upwards, your wrist is said to be in a *Kayâ* (Supine) position. In many Cebuano systems this position is known as *Hayáng*.

Kulob

When your palm is facing the ground, your wrist is said to be in a *Kulob* (Prone) position.

When striking (#1 or #3) from an *Abierta* (open) position, your weapon starts in, and makes contact with the target, while your wrist is in a *Kayâ* (supine) position (Fig. 1). After contact is made and the strike is completed, the wrist is flipped into a *Kulob* (prone) position.

When striking (#2 or #4) from a *Serrada* (closed) position, your weapon starts in, and makes contact with the target, while your wrist is in a *Kulob* (prone) position (Fig. 2). After contact is made and the strike is completed, the wrist is flipped into a *Kayâ* (supine) position.

It is important to note that when thrusting at the chest, the position of the wrist is reversed, so that a #5 thrust to the chest starts from the *Abierta* guard in a *Kulob* position (Fig. 3). Whereas a #6 thrust to the chest starts from the *Serrada* guard in a *Kayâ* position (Fig. 4).

GARÁHE

The term *Garáhe* literally translates as "garage" and in Bernas Estocadas refers to positions in which the stick is parked, rested or chambered on the shoulders (Fig. 1 & 2) or arm (Fig. 3). These parked positions are used both in drills and in combative applications.

1. Garáhe over right shoulder
2. Garáhe over left shoulder
3. Garáhe over left arm

PIGAR AND THE NGANGÁNG BUÁYA

Pigar means to "push" and is a key feature of many of the blocking and striking techniques in Bernas Estocadas. It is used to push the opponent away, or to limit their movements, in preparation for a strike or counter (see Fig. 1).

Figure 3 and 4 below, both show the *Pigar* as a kind of protective parry that accompanies a striking action. *Pigar* may also be used to control or jam the opponent's limbs after a block, often in preparation for grabbing with the *Ngangáng Buáya* or 'Crocodile Mouth' (see Fig. 2). Figures 5, 6 & 7 also demonstrate the *Pigar* following what are blocking motions in Bernas Estocadas, in preparation for a counterstrike or disarm. In each case the *Pigar* is ready to transform into the *Ngangáng Buáya*, snapping shut *(Kagát)* around the opponent's weapon arm, the thumb and fingers creating the jaws of the crocodile.

2
PANÍNDOG
STANCES

PANÍNDOG

There are five fundamental stances in the Bernas Estocadas system:

- HILÁY LIKÓD - Back Stance
- HILÁY TUBANG - Forward Stance
- BAKÂ - Horse Stance
- PÚNGKÒ - Cat Stance
- EKIS - Cross Stance

The stances ensure good form, balance, foot position, and effective weight distribution are taught as a core aspect of the art.

To practice the stances, there is an 8-Count routine that is performed, set out in the table below. Start in *Preparar* (with your right foot forward), then *Garáhe* (park) your stick over your right shoulder. Then for each count, follow the advice in the table below.

Stances	Stationary				Advancing		Retreating	
	1	2	3	4	5	6	7	8
HILÁY LIKÓD Back Stance	Advance	Retreat	Advance	Retreat	Advance	Advance	Retreat	Retreat
HILÁY TUBANG Forward Stance	Advance	Retreat	Advance	Retreat	Advance	Advance	Retreat	Retreat
BAKÂ Horse Stance	Advance	Retreat	Advance	Retreat	Advance	Advance	Retreat	Retreat
PÚNGKÒ Cat Stance	Retreat	Advance	Retreat	Advance	Advance	Advance	Retreat	Retreat
EKIS Cross Stance	Retreat	Advance	Retreat	Advance	Advance	Advance	Retreat	Retreat

EXAMPLE OF HOW TO PERFORM THE PANÍNDOG ROUTINE

Here is how the *Paníndog* routine is performed using *Hiláy Likód* (Back Stance) as an example:

1. For the first count, start by advancing with your left leg into a left-side leading Back Stance;
2. For the second count, withdraw your left leg into a right-side leading Back Stance;
3. For the third count, advance again with your left leg into a left-side leading Back Stance; and
4. For the fourth count, again withdraw your left leg into a right-side leading Back Stance.
5. For the fifth count, advance again with your left leg into a left-side leading Back Stance;
6. For the sixth count, advance with your right leg into a right-side leading Back Stance;
7. For the seventh count, retreat with your right leg into a left-side leading Back Stance; and
8. For the eighth and final count, retreat with your left leg into a right-side leading Back Stance.

This completes the *Paníndog* routine for Back Stance. The first four counts complete the "stationary" aspect of the drill, because you are really just shuffling forward and back without really moving from the same spot. The fifth and sixth counts complete the "advancing" aspect of the drill; and the seventh and eighth counts complete the "retreating" aspect of the drill.

The purpose of this routine is to get you used to moving between stances, and also maintaining good form as you move.

HILÁY LIKÓD | BACK STANCE

To assume a back stance, step to the rear with your left or right leg. Your feet should assume a loose 'L' shape, with your lead foot pointing towards your imaginary opponent. Your body leans to the rear, with approximately 70% of your weight on the rear leg, and 30% of your weight on the lead leg. Your torso is 'bladed' by turning slightly to the side, giving an opponent in front of you less of a target.

HILÁY TUBANG | FORWARD STANCE

To assume a forward stance, step forward with your left or right leg. Your feet should assume a loose 'L' shape, with your lead foot pointing towards your imaginary opponent. Your body is centred over your lead leg, with approximately 70% of your weight on the lead leg, and 30% of your weight on the rear leg. Your torso is 'bladed' by turning slightly to the side, giving an opponent in front of you less of a target. You can switch easily between a Forward Stance and Back Stance just by turning and looking in the opposite direction, without shifting weight distribution.

View from the open side

View from the blindside

View from the front

BAKÂ | HORSE STANCE

Bakâ literally means "to straddle", and to assume a Horse Stance, divide your weight evenly between both legs, and lower your body as if riding a horse. Your feet will still form a loose 'L' shape as if you are standing on two sides of a square. Your torso is, like the Back Stance, slightly 'bladed' or turned side on relative to the opponent.

View from the open side

View from the blindside

View from the front

PÚNGKÒ | CAT STANCE

Púnkò literally means "to be seated", and so to assume the Cat Stance, all the weight is shifted to one leg, and the other leg lighty rests on either the ball of the foot with heel up, or the outside edge of the foot, with the knees bent as if you are sitting on a stool. Because the feet are close together, the Cat Stance facilitates fast switching of direction.

Front view
Weight on left leg

Front view
Weight on right leg

Side view
Weight on right leg

Side view
Weight on left leg

EKIS | CROSS STANCE

The Cross Stance is used for advancing or retreating, and can also facilitate the fast changing of directions. To advance with the Cross Stance, the left leg steps behind the right leg. To retreat, the right leg steps in front of the left leg. Your weight is distributed almost evenly once you are in the Cross Stance position. Your body should also be lowered so that your legs are well bent.

View from the open side

View from the front

View from the open side
Counterbalancing with arm and weapon

3
PALAKÁT
FOOTWORK

FOOTWORK DRILLS

One of the first things you may notice about Bernas Estocadas is that a practitioner of this system will always be moving. Footwork is synchronised with every strike and block from the very beginning. As the art has a specific focus on handling multiple opponents, multi-directional footwork is an essential and standout feature of the system. The student of Bernas Estocadas will learn to strike and block while moving laterally, as well as advancing and retreating.

STANDARD FOOTWORK TEMPLATE

The standard footwork template is used for many of the drills in Bernas Estocadas, including *Palakát* (footwork), *Paníndog* (stance), *Opensa* (striking), *Depensa* (blocking), and *Páres Páres* (paired striking and blocking) training routines.

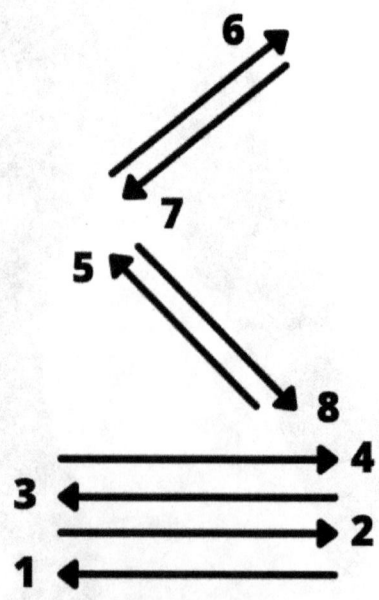

When performing a routine using the standard footwork template, repetitions 1-4 involve moving side-to-side, repetition 5 & 6 involve advancing to the left and right, and repetition 7 & 8 involve retreating to the left and right.

OPENSA PALAKÁT 1 & 2

Footwork for Opensa 1 & 2 involves a double-step action. Start in Cat Stance with weight on the right leg (Fig. 1). When stepping left, the left foot moves first (using the stationary right leg as a base to push off from). When the left foot reaches its destination the weight shifts to the left foot, and the right foot catches up into a Cat Stance (Fig. 2). These directions are reversed when stepping back to the right. Switch your stick from shoulder to shoulder (tip up) as you step.

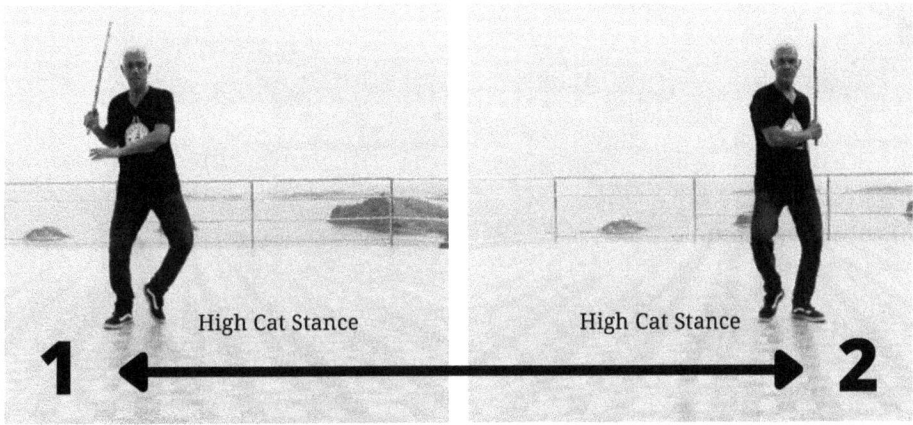

OPENSA PALAKÁT 3 & 4

The footwork for Opensa 3 & 4 is identical to that used for 1 & 2, with the exception that you should bend your knees more, and adopt a lower stance throughout the stepping action; and the stick is kept low (tip down) while shifting side to side with your stepping.

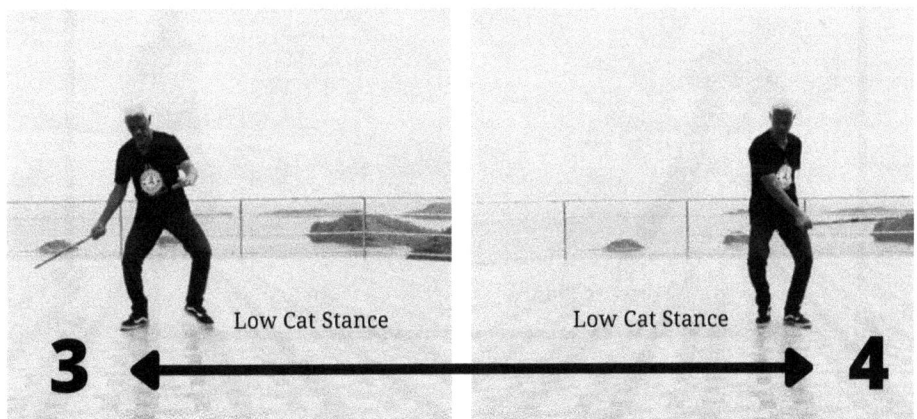

OPENSA PALAKÁT 5 & 6

To practice the footwork for Opensa 5, start in a Cat Stance with your weight on your right leg (Fig. 1). When moving left, step out with the left foot into a Forward Stance, shifting your weapon from an *Abierta* position to a *Serrada* position (Fig. 2). To perform the footwork for Opensa 6, shift all your weight onto your left leg forming another Cat Stance (Fig. 3), then step out with your right leg into a Forward Stance, shifting your weapon from a *Serrada* position to an *Abierta* position.

OPENSA PALAKÁT 7 & 8

When practicing the footwork for Opensa 7, you step back into Cat Stance when retreating, with the weight on your left leg (Fig. 1a). If advancing with Opensa 7 you step into Cross Stance with the weight on your right leg (Fig. 1b). When advancing or retreating with Opensa 8, you move directly into a Forward Stance with the weight on the right leg (dropping the stick for Opensa 7 and raising it for Opensa 8).

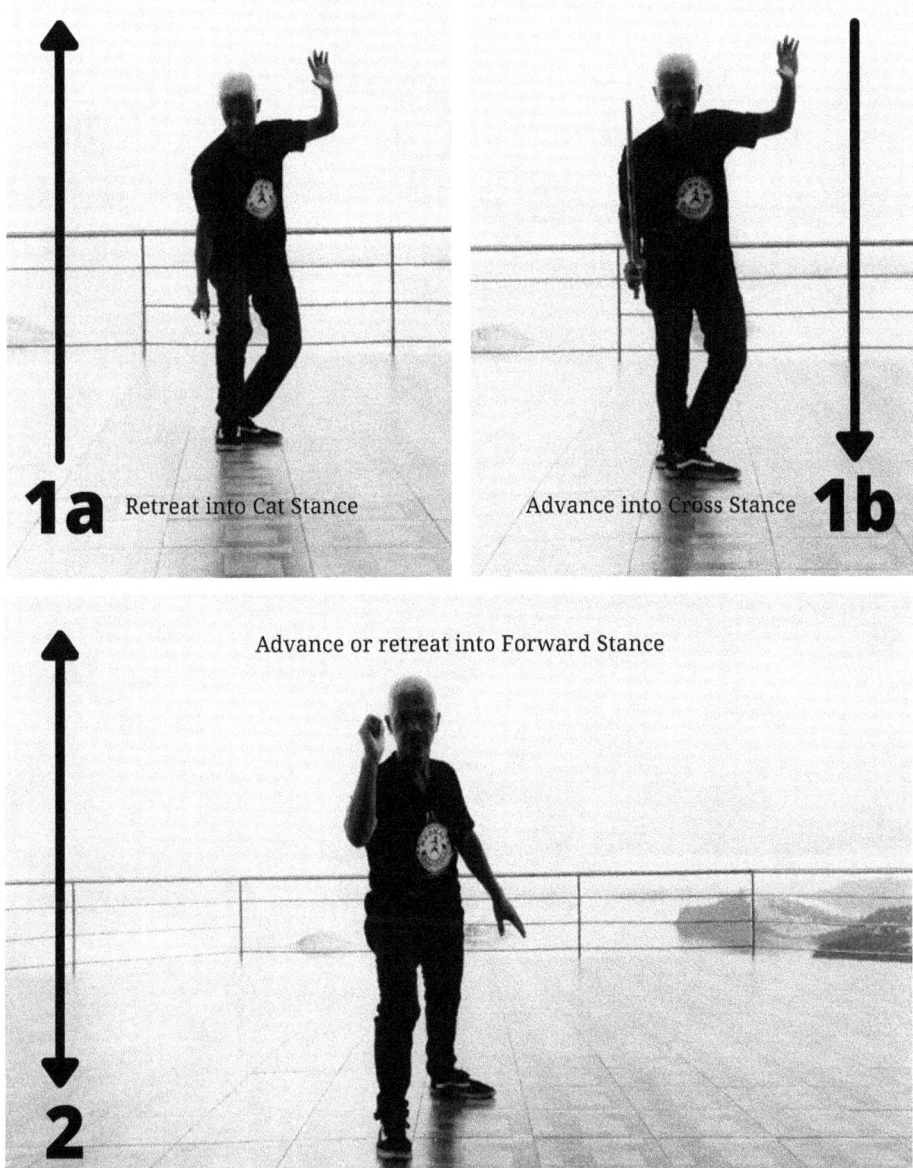

1a Retreat into Cat Stance
1b Advance into Cross Stance
2 Advance or retreat into Forward Stance

OPENSA PALAKÁT 9 & 10

To practice footwork for Opensa 9, step to your left with your left foot landing with the heel first, and shifting your weapon from *Abierta* to *Serrada* (Fig. 1), then as you shift your weight onto your left leg, pivot into a Cat Stance facing to the right (Fig. 2). For Opensa 10, step with your right foot to the right, placing your heel on the ground first, and shifting your weapon from *Serrada* to *Abierta* (Fig. 3), then as you shift your weight onto the right leg, pivot into a Cat Stance facing the left (Fig. 4).

OPENSA PALAKÁT 11 & 12

For Opensa 11, retreat by stepping your right leg in front of your left leg forming a Cross Stance, with your weapon held low (Fig. 1a & 1b). For Opensa 12, step forward with your right leg into a Forward Stance, with your weapon parked on your right shoulder (Fig. 2).

Cross Stance (Front View)

1a

Forward Stance

2

Cross Stance (Side View)

1b

4
OPENSA
12 STRIKES

OPENSA

Bernas Estocadas has series of 12 Strikes that form the foundational *Opensa* (offensive methods) of the system. Each of the 12 Strikes follows a specific angle of attack, is synchronised with specific footwork, and is aimed at a specific target (though as the student progresses into the *Pang-Áway* combative applications of the system, there is some flexibility that arises in terms of targeting, trajectory being privileged).

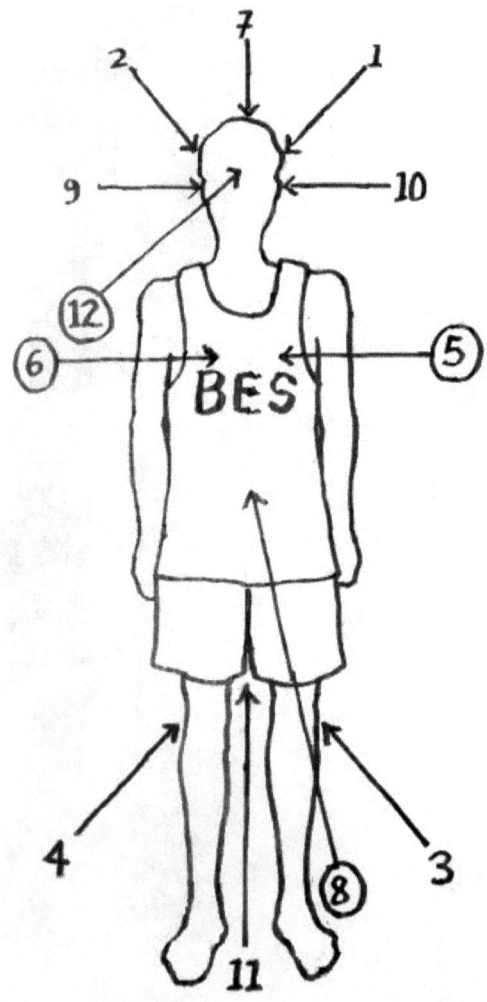

Diagram of the 12 Strikes and their Intended Targets

GEOMETRY OF THE OPENSA

The first four strikes in Bernas Estocadas form a multiplication sign. The diagram below shows the first four angles of attack as viewed from the perspective of the person throwing the strikes.

OPENSA 1-4

The first four strikes in Bernas Estocadas form a multiplication sign. Opensa 1 & 2 are called *Tapás* or "tree-felling" strikes, executed as if you are chopping the trunk of a banana tree with your *Talíbong*. While Opensa 3 & 4 are called *Hágbas* or "grass-cutting" strikes, executed with a scooping action as if trying to lop the top off some weeds.

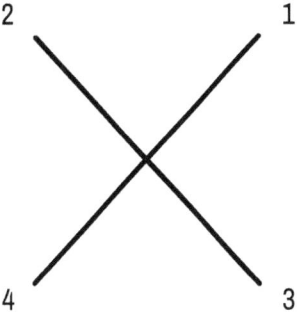

OPENSA 5-8

The second group of four strikes in Bernas Estocadas form a plus sign. Opensa 5, 6 & 8 are *Totsada* or "thrusts"; while Opensa 7 is called *Dagdag* meaning to drop or strike straight down.

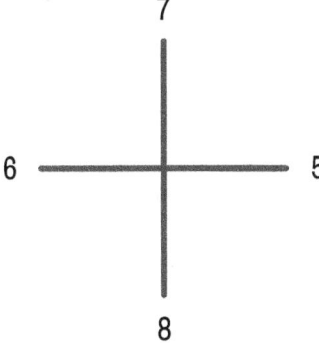

OPENSA 9-12

The third group of four strikes in Bernas Estocadas also form a plus sign. Opensa 9 is called *Waslik* because it is a horizontal backhand that "strikes to the rear". Opensa 10 is called *Labô* as it is a standard forehand horizontal strike or slash. Opensa 11 is called *Witik* which means to flip or flick, as it is an upward strike to the groin. Finally, Opensa 12 as a thrust to the face, is also a *Totsada*.

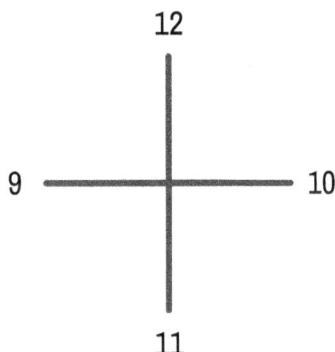

TYPES OF STRIKES

In Bernas Estocadas we distinguish between three types of strikes:

- A *De Pondo* strike stops when it meets its intended target. These strikes usually have stopping force, transmitting their force at the point of impact; the equivalent of chopping with a blade. *De Pondo* strikes are also used when feeding attacks in the first stages of *Opensa-Depensa* (Attack and Defence) training, and are frequently used in the blocking techniques of the *12 Depensa*.

- A *Derecho* strike passes all the way through its intended target. This is the standard way of executing most strikes, and is the equivalent of slashing with a blade. It is often used as a finishing blow, and in such instances may be combined with a *Túmbada* action in which the strike is delivered all the way to the ground. It is also seen in *Redonda* or circular strikes, that start and end in the same location, but travel through a full striking arc.

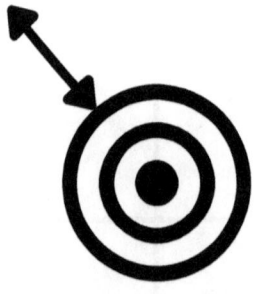

- A *De Lástiko* strike snaps back to its starting position after it meets the target. This type of striking is the equivalent of a Boxer's jab. It facilitates rapid directional changes, and can be seen in techniques like *Abaníko* or fanning motions

PALABÚLAK

There are four additional types of strikes in Bernas Estocadas, that form part of the *Pang-Áway* combatives curriculum, and will be addressed more fully in a future volume. *Palabúlak* means "flowering" and these strikes add a flourish to the striking methods of the system. The *Palabúlak* of Bernas Estocadas are:

WASIWAS
Wasiwas means to wave to and fro, to brandish, or to wag (like a dog's tail). It is a low horizontal strike that whips side to side.

PÁLPAL
Pálpal means to stake or peg (like bashing a tent peg into the ground). It involves striking down on top of the opponent's head or hands using the flat side of your blade.

ABANÍKO
Abaníko means to fan. A fanning strike uses the forearm as an axis around which to rotate rapidly from side to side.

REDONDA
Redonda means round. A redonda strike starts and finishes in the same location, having whipped through a complete circular arc.

At advanced levels, these four *Palabúlak* are combined with the *Opensa* to create dynamic and unpredictable fighting combinations.

Application of Opensa 1
Tapás Downward Diagonal Forehand Strike to Temple

OPENSA 1

Opensa 1 is a downward diagonal forehand strike to the opponent's left temple. Start in Cat Stance while chambering your weapon over your right shoulder and executing a *Pigar* with your left hand (Fig. 1). Then, as you step to the left, execute your downward diagonal forehand strike (Fig. 2 & 3). Finish in a Cat Stance with your weapon chambered beside your left shoulder (Fig. 4).

Application of Opensa 2
Tapás Downward Diagonal Backhand Strike to Temple

OPENSA 2

Opensa 2 is a downward diagonal backhand strike to the opponent's right temple. Start in Cat Stance while chambering your weapon over your left shoulder with your left arm by your side (Fig. 1). Then, as you step to the right, execute your downward diagonal backhand strike (Fig. 2, 3 & 4). Finish in a Cat Stance with your weapon chambered over your right shoulder and your left hand executing a *Pigar* (Fig. 5).

Application of Opensa 3
Hagbás Upward Diagonal Forehand Strike to Knee

OPENSA 3

Opensa 3 is an upward diagonal forehand strike to the opponent's knees. Start in a deep Cat Stance while chambering your weapon beside your right shoulder and executing a *Pigar* with your left hand (Fig. 1). Then, as you step to the left, your left hand sweeps to the rear (as a potential parry) while you scoop upwards with your weapon to execute your strike (Fig. 2 & 3). Finish in a Cat Stance with your weapon level with your left elbow (Fig. 4).

Application of Opensa 4
Hagbás Upward Diagonal Backhand Strike to Knee

OPENSA 4

Opensa 4 is an upward diagonal backhand strike to the opponent's knees. Start in a deep Cat Stance while chambering your weapon beside your left shoulder with your left arm by your side (Fig. 1). Then, as you step to the right push forward with your left arm to help launch your upward diagonal strike (Fig. 2 & 3). Finish in a deep Cat Stance with your weapon beside your right shoulder and your left hand *Pigar* (Fig. 4).

Application of Opensa 5
Totsada Palm Down Thrust to Chest

OPENSA 5

Start in Cat Stance in an *Abierta* position with your weapon pointing at the opponent, your wrist in a *Kulob* (prone) position, and your left hand executing a *Pigar* (Fig. 1). As you step to the left, parry lateral and downwards with your left hand (Fig. 2), and thrust to your left aiming at your opponent's chest (Fig. 3 & 4). Finish in a Forward Stance as your thrust meets its target (Fig. 5)

Application of Opensa 6
Totsada Palm Up Thrust to Chest

OPENSA 6

Start in Cat Stance in an *Serrada* position with your weapon pointing at the opponent, your wrist in a *Kayâ* (supine) position, and your left hand guarding the right side of your neck and chest (Fig. 1). As you step to the right, parry lateral and downwards with your left hand (Fig. 2 & 3), and thrust to your right aiming at your opponent's chest (Fig. 3 & 4). Finish in a Forward Stance as your thrust meets its target (Fig. 4)

Application of Opensa 7
Dagdag Direct Downward Strike to Crown of Head

OPENSA 7

From *Preparar* (Fig. 1), shift your weight into a Forward Stance while chambering your weapon high (Fig. 2), then, while shifting your weight onto your right leg, step your left foot forward just in front of your right, so you are in a Cat Stance (Fig. 3) and strike straight downwards while bringing your left hand upwards to protect your head (Fig. 4).

Application of Opensa 8
Totsada Direct Thrust to Torso

OPENSA 8

From Cat Stance with your weight on your left leg and your *Pigar* protectiong your head (Fig. 1), step forward with your right foot (Fig. 2); then as you shift your weight onto your right leg (Fig. 3), move into a Forward Stance while thrusting your weapon at your opponent's torso and counterbalancing by parrying downwards and to the rear (Fig. 4).

Application of Opensa 9
Wáslik Horizontal Backhand Strike to Head

OPENSA 9

Start in Cat Stance with your weight on your right leg and your weapon in a *Serrada* position (Fig. 1). Step to your left (Fig. 2). Then start turning your body to the right (Fig. 3) as you parry first (Fig. 4), then extend your horizontal strike (Fig. 5). Your *Waslik* style strike terminates as it meets your opponent's neck, and you enter Cat Stance with weight on your left leg.

Application of Opensa 10
Labô Horizontal Forehand Strike to Head

OPENSA 10

Start in Cat Stance with your weight on your left leg and your weapon in an *Abierta* position (Fig. 1). Step to your right (Fig. 2). Then start turning your body to the left as you parry with your left hand to clear the path (Fig. 3), for your *Labô* style strike that terminates as it meets your opponent's neck, and you enter Cat Stance with weight on your right leg (Fig. 4).

Application of Opensa 11
Witik Upward Backhand Strike to Groin

OPENSA 11

Opensa 11 can be performed with two different kinds of footwork and stances. The first option is to simply step rearward with your left foot into your Back Stance, weapon in a *Serrada* position (Fig. 1a). Then parry underneath your weapon arm while swinging upward with your strike towards the groin (Fig. 2a).

The second option is to advance by stepping forward with your right leg while chambering your weapon in a high *Serrada* position (Fig. 1b). Then stepping forward with your left leg behind your right leg into a Cross Stance, as you hit upwards towards the groin with your weapon (Fig. 2b). It is also possible to retreat with this method, stepping with the right foot in front of the left.

Application of Opensa 12
Totsada Palm Up Thrust to Eyes

OPENSA 12

From Cat Stance with your weight on your left leg and your weapon hand in a *Kayâ* (Supine) position in a *Serrada* stance (Fig. 1), parry downwards and rearwards with your left hand (as if stroking a cat you are holding in your right arm) as you step forward (Fig. 2 & 3), finishing in a Forward Stance as you thrust towards your opponent's eyes (Fig. 4).

5
DEPENSA
12 BLOCKS

DEPENSA

In the Bernas Estocadas system there are 12 Blocks (or defences), that match up with the 12 Strikes. Each block is paired with its corresponding strike (see Chapter 8 Opensa-Depensa). For now, the *Depensa* are practiced as a solo technical drill (though we have included an image for each of the 12 blocks that shows its application to help you visualise what you are trying to defend against).

ALKONTRA KARGADA

The core principle of the *Depensa* is expressed by the term *Alkontra Kargada*, which is an idiom that means to "meet the force". In basic training, this is achieved by blocking via weapon to weapon contact. In essence *Alkontra Kargada* is a way of attacking the attack, striking it off-course to create an opportunity for your own counterattack.

SAGÁNG

In Ilonggo, *Sagáng* means to prevent, forestall, ward off, stop, or parry. In Bernas Estocadas it is a general term for "blocking". There are three basic types of blocks that occur repeatedly within the *Depensa*. The three types of blocks utilise the following principles or mechanics:

De Pondo (anchoring) type blocks strike the opponent's weapon back in the direction from which it originated. They occur in Depensa 1, 2, 3, 6, & 10 (tip of the weapon pointing upwards) and in Depensa 4 & 11 (tip of the weapon pointing downwards).

Páyong (umbrella) type blocks use the defender's weapon as a shield to protect them as they knock the attack off-course. They occur in Depensa 5 & 9.

Wáslik (whipping) blocks use a rearward flicking motion to strike the opponent's attack off-course. They occur in Depensa 7, 8, & 12, all centreline attacks.

TÍEMPO (TYEMPO)

In Ilonggo, *Tíempo* refers to time or timing. In Bernas Estocadas three different temporal moments are identified that determine the mode of counterattack.

Antis means "before" and may be thought about as an "attack on preparation". In practice, this means anticipating the opponent's intent, and initiating your counter the moment you see them prepare to attack, before they have had a chance to launch their offensive manoeuvre.

Oramismo means "at the same time", and may be thought about as "attacking the attack". The fundamental *Depensa* in Bernas Estocadas are practiced in an *Oramismo Tíempo*. In other words, you execute your *Depensa* in precisely the same timing as the opponent launches their attack, as if perfectly synchronised with each other.

Tapos means "after" and may be thought about as an "attack on completion". In practice, this means evading the opponent's attack and waiting till it has missed its intended target, before executing your own counterattack.

NGANGÁNG BUÁYA

Another important aspect of the *Depensa*, is the active use of the "alive hand" or *Ngangáng Buáya* (crocodile mouth) in actions such as *Pigar* (pushing), or *Kagát* (biting). The alive hand and weapon form an important partnership in each of the *12 Depensa*. To completely understand the function and movement of the alive hand, review the information in Chapter 1 (where *Pigar* and the *Ngangáng Buáya* were introduced), in Chapter 7 (where its movements are synchronised with the striking and blocking techniques), and in Chapter 8 (where its function and application is demonstrated throughout the *Opensa-Depensa* drill).

Application of Depensa 1
High Inside De Pondo Block

DEPENSA 1

Against a downward diagonal forehand strike to the temple (Opensa 1), step diagonally forward to your right (Fig. 2), while using a *De Pondo* forehand block to the opponent's weapon to stop it in its tracks (Fig. 3), almost simultaneously execute your *Pigar* over the top of your weapon arm, catching the opponent's hand with your *Ngangáng Buáya* thumb downwards while finishing in a Forward Stance (Fig. 4).

Application of Depensa 2
High Outside De Pondo Block

DEPENSA 2

Against a downward diagonal backhand strike to the temple (Opensa 2), step diagonally forward to your left (Fig. 2), while using a *De Pondo* backhand block to the opponent's weapon to stop it in its tracks (Fig. 3), simultaneously applying a *Pigar* to the opponent's hand, then catching the opponent's hand with your *Ngangáng Buáya* thumb downwards, while finishing in a Forward Stance (Fig. 4).

Application of Depensa 3
Low Inside De Pondo Block

DEPENSA 3

Against an upward diagonal forehand strike to your knee (Opensa 3), step diagonally forward to your right (Fig. 2), while striking downwards using a *De Pondo* forehand block to the opponent's weapon to stop it in its tracks (Fig. 3), applying your Pigar over the top of your weapon arm, and catching the opponent's hand with your *Ngangáng Buáya* with thumb downwards, terminating in a Horse Stance (Fig. 4).

Application of Depensa 4
Low Outside De Pondo Block

DEPENSA 4

Against an upward diagonal forehand strike to your knee (Opensa 4), step diagonally forward to your right (Fig. 2), while striking downwards using a *De Pondo* backhand block to the opponent's weapon to stop it in its tracks (Fig. 3), applying your *Pigar* to the opponent's arm, then catching the opponent's hand with your *Ngangáng Buáya* with thumb upwards, terminating in a Forward Stance (Fig. 4).

Application of Depensa 5
Inside Payong Block

DEPENSA 5

Against a palm down thrust to your chest (Opensa 5), step diagonally forward to your right (Fig. 2), while bringing your weapon up and across your body in a *Páyong* block (tip facing downwards) to deflect the thrust off its course (Fig. 3), applying your *Pigar*, then catching the opponent's hand with your *Ngangáng Buáya* thumb upwards, terminating in a Forward Stance (Fig. 4).

Application of Depensa 6
Outside Mid-Level De Pondo Block

DEPENSA 6

Against a palm up thrust to your chest (Opensa 6), while chambering your weapon over your left shoulder (Fig. 2), step diagonally forward to your left (Fig. 3), then using a *De Pondo* block, knock the thrust off course, simultaneously applying your *Pigar*, then catching the opponent's hand with your *Ngangáng Buáya* thumb downwards, terminating in a Forward Stance (Fig. 4).

Application of Depensa 7
Mid-Level Waslik Block

DEPENSA 7

Against a downward strike to the crown of your head (Opensa 7), chamber your weapon over your left shoulder (Fig. 2), then keeping your stick with the tip pointing upwards, deflect the attack off its course by striking it to the side with a backhand *Waslik* block (Fig. 3), simultaneously applying your *Pigar*, then catching the opponent's hand with your *Ngangáng Buáya* thumb downwards, maintaining a right foot lead position (Fig. 4).

Application of Depensa 8
Low Waslik Block

DEPENSA 8

Against a thrust to your stomach (Opensa 8), step diagonally forward to the left while raising your weapon (Fig. 2). As you shift weight onto your left foot, aim your *Punyo* (butt of your stick) at the in-coming weapon (Fig. 3). Then deflect the thrust by striking their weapon aside using a *Waslik* (rearward whipping action), simultaneously applying your *Pigar*, then catching the opponent's hand with your *Ngangáng Buáya* thumb upwards, as you terminate your motion in a Forward Stance (Fig. 4).

Application of Depensa 8
High Outside Payong Block

DEPENSA 9

Against a horizontal backhand strike to the side of your face or neck (Opensa 9), step forward with your right foot, allowing your weapon to chamber your over your left shoulder by raising your *Punyo* (Fig. 2). As you duck, meet the opponent's weapon with your own stick in *Páyong* (umbrella) fashion while following their weapon's path with your *Pigar* to glide it off your stick (Fig. 3). Then catch hold of the opponent's hand with your *Ngangáng Buáya* thumb downwards, terminating in a Forward Stance (Fig. 4). Your weapon may terminate in a *Túmbada* strike to the ground.

Application of Depensa 10
Mid-Level Inside De Pondo Block

DEPENSA 10

Against a horizontal forehand strike to the side of your face or neck (Opensa 10), step forward with your left foot, allowing your weapon to chamber your over your right shoulder by raising your *Punyo* (Fig. 2). Then turn to meet the opponent's weapon while stepping to the left (Fig. 3), with a mid-level inside *De Pondo* block, tip pointing upwards, shoot your *Pigar* over the top of your own arm, catching hold of the opponent's hand with your *Ngangáng Buáya* thumb downwards, terminating in a Forward Stance (Fig. 4).

Application of Depensa 11
Low Outside De Pondo Block

DEPENSA 11

Against an upward backhand strike to your groin (Opensa 11), rock your weight onto your left leg while chambering your weapon over your left shoulder (Fig. 2). Then shifting your weight onto your right leg, snap your weapon diagonally forward and downward almost in a rowing-like action (Fig. 3). As you knock their strike back with your *De Pondo* block, shoot your *Pigar* over the top of your own arm, then catch the opponent's hand with your *Nganging Buáya* thumb upwards, terminating in a Forward Stance (Fig. 4).

Application of Depensa 12
High Waslik Block

DEPENSA 12

Against a palm up thrust towards your eyes (Opensa 12), chamber your weapon over your left shoulder as you shift your weight onto your right foot (Fig. 2). Then stepping diagonally forward with your left foot, and keeping your stick with the tip pointing upwards, deflect the attack off its course by striking it to the side using a *Waslik* motion (Fig. 3). As you complete your *Waslik* motion, and simultaneous *Pigar*, catch the opponent's hand with your *Ngangáng Buáya* thumb downwards, maintaining a left foot lead Forward Stance (Fig. 4).

6
PÁRES PÁRES
PAIRED STRIKES AND BLOCKS

OPENSA PÁRES PÁRES

Opensa Páres Páres (Offensive Pairs) is a key method of drilling the 12 Strikes in "paired" groupings as follows:

- 1 + 2
- 3 + 4
- 5 + 6
- 7 + 8
- 9 + 10
- 11 + 12

Completing *Opensa Páres Páres* involves eight repetitions of each pair of strikes, using the standard footwork template (repeated in the diagram below), where the first four repetitions are performed side to side, the fifth and sixth repetitions are performed while advancing, and the seventh and eighth repetitions are performed while retreating.

**STANDARD FOOTWORK TEMPLATE
FOR OPENSA PARES PARES**

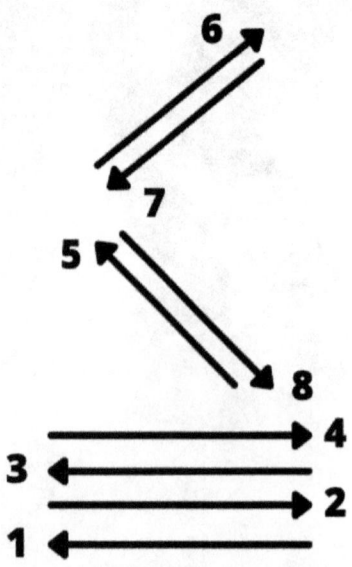

PASUNÓD OPENSA

A second method of performing the paired groupings is known as *Pasunód Opensa* (Consecutive Strikes). In the *Pasunód Opensa* drill you execute the strikes in the following groupings:

- 1-2
- 1-2 + 3-4
- 1-2 + 3-4 + 5-6
- 1-2 + 3-4+ 5-6 + 7-8
- 1-2 + 3-4+ 5-6 + 7-8 + 9-10
- 1-2 + 3-4+ 5-6 + 7-8 + 9-10 + 11-12

Each grouping is performed four times. The first repetition should be slow and smooth. The second repetition should be a little quicker. The third repetition executed faster again with power and intention. The final repetition should be executed with full power, speed and intention. You should hear your stick cutting the air.

These *Pasunód Opensa* consecutive striking sequences are performed on the spot. There is no advancing or retreating required. You simply execute the techniques moving side to side, first to the left, and then to the right.

TRIANGLE FOOTWORK FOR PASUNÓD OPENSA

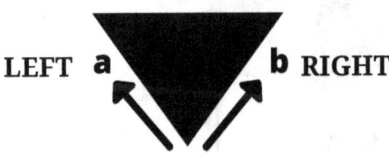

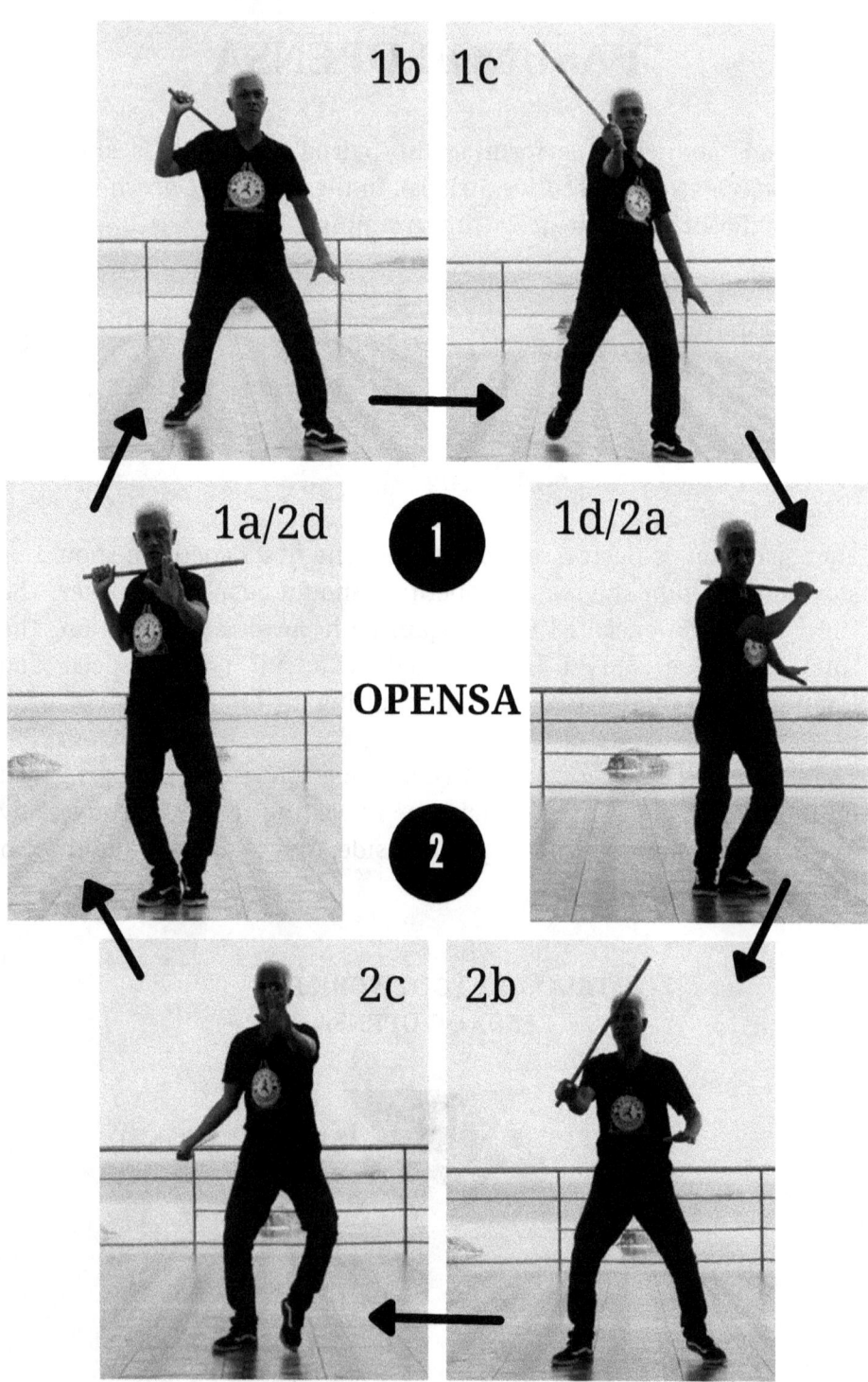

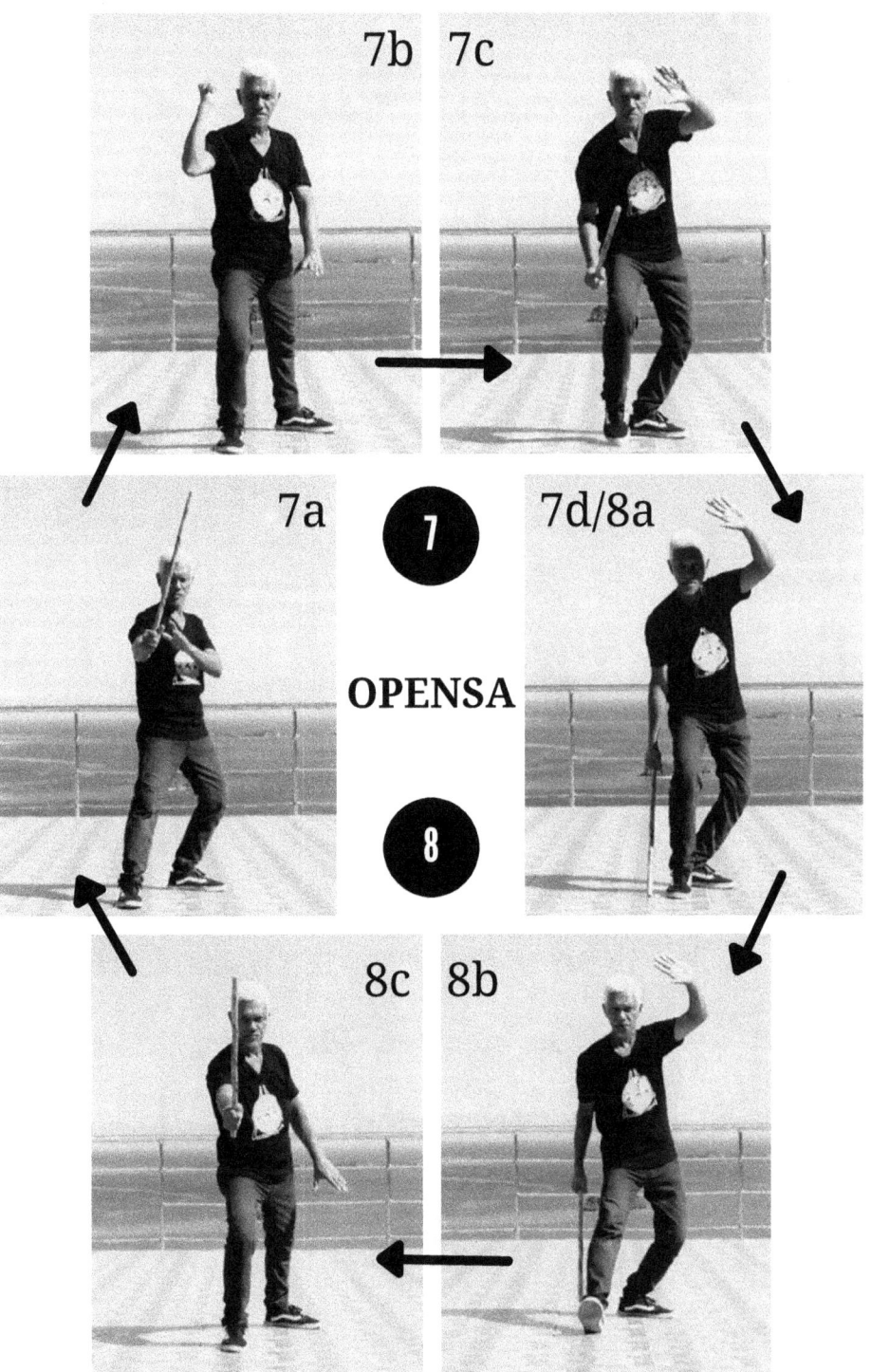

PASUNÓD TAGDUHÁ

A third method of performing the paired groupings is called *Pasunód Tagduhá* (Consecutive Two-Strike Combinations). Although a more advanced drill forming part of the *Pang-Áway* (Combatives) curriculum, *Pasunód Tagduhá* builds easily on the *Páres Páres* structure.

Each combination should be executed advancing (twice) and retreating (twice), while maintaining your orientation to an imaginary opponent in front of you. The letter 'a' represents the first strike, and the letter 'b' represents the second strike, in each combination. The arrows suggest the angle of each step made.

Each combination should be executed with full power, speed and intention. You should hear your stick cutting the air.

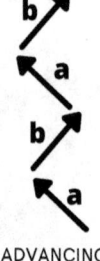
ADVANCING

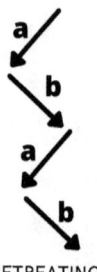
RETREATING

LEVEL ONE
Practice in the following standard combinations:

- 1 + 2
- 2 + 3
- 3 + 4
- 4 + 5
- 5 + 6
- 6 + 7
- 7 + 8
- 8 + 9
- 9 + 10
- 10 + 11
- 11 + 12

LEVEL TWO
Practice in the following mirrored combinations:

- 1 + 2 then 2 + 1
- 2 + 3 then 3 + 2
- 3 + 4 then 4 + 3
- 4 + 5 then 5 + 4
- 5 + 6 then 6 + 5
- 6 + 7 then 7 + 6
- 7 + 8 then 8 + 7
- 8 + 9 then 9 + 8
- 9 + 10 then 10 + 9
- 10 + 11 then 11 + 10
- 11 + 12 then 12 + 11

DEPENSA PÁRES PÁRES

Depensa Páres Páres (Defensive Pairs) is a key method of drilling the 12 Blocks in "paired" groupings as follows:

- 1 + 2
- 3 + 4
- 5 + 6
- 7 + 8
- 9 + 10
- 11 + 12

Completing *Depensa Páres Páres* involves eight repetitions of each pair of blocks, using the footwork templates opposite. Each repetition of a "pair" of blocks is executed either advancing or retreating:

- Repetition 1, 3, 5 & 6 are performed advancing.
- Repetition 2, 4, 7 & 8 are performed retreating.

Note, that Bernas Estocadas does not advocate continuous blocking. This exercise is simply a drill to build fluidity. As you become proficient with the Depensa, it will be become obvious that the blocks themselves are designed to strike the opponent's weapon off its trajectory, rather than being some kind of passive barrier between the opponent's weapon and its target.

8-COUNT, EACH REPETITION
EQUALS ONE PAIR OF BLOCKS

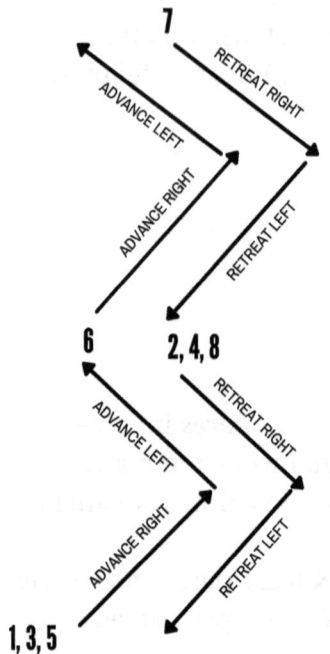

8-COUNT, EACH REPETITION
EQUALS ONE BLOCK

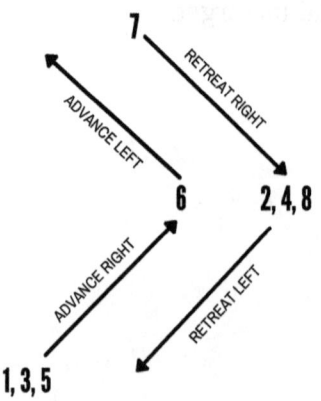

PASUNÓD DEPENSA

A second method of performing the paired groupings is known as *Pasunód Opensa* (Consecutive Strikes) and *Pasunód Depensa* (Consecutive Blocks). In the Pasunod drill you execute the strikes and blocks in the following groupings:

- 1-2
- 1-2 + 3-4
- 1-2 + 3-4 + 5-6
- 1-2 + 3-4+ 5-6 + 7-8
- 1-2 + 3-4+ 5-6 + 7-8 + 9-10
- 1-2 + 3-4+ 5-6 + 7-8 + 9-10 + 11-12

Each grouping is performed four times. The first repetition should be slow and smooth. The second repetition should be a little quicker. The third repetition executed faster again with power and intention. The final repetition should be executed with full power, speed and intention. You should hear your stick cutting the air.

These *Pasunód Depensa* consecutive blocking sequences are performed on the spot. There is no advancing or retreating required. You simply execute the techniques moving side to side using a triangular stepping pattern where 'a' represents the first step, and 'b' represents the second step, in each pair of blocks. Again, it is important to note this is a drill to build fluidity of movement between positions. Bernas Estocadas does not advocate continuous blocking, but rather moving from your block immediately into a counterstrike, as is seen in our chapter on *Opensa-Depensa* (Attack-Defence).

**TRIANGLE FOOTWORK FOR
PASUNÓD DEPENSA**

BERNAS ESTOCADAS

DEPENSA 1

DEPENSA

2

DEPENSA

3

4 DEPENSA

BERNAS ESTOCADAS

5

DEPENSA

6 DEPENSA

7
DEPENSA

8 DEPENSA

9 DEPENSA

10 DEPENSA

DEPENSA

12 DEPENSA

7
DÁGWAY
FORMS

DÁGWAY

The *Dágway* are the "forms" used in Bernas Estocadas, often referred to as *Anyo* in other systems. These forms not only teach you to move, strike and block in multiple directions, they reveal the system's emphasis on learning to handle multiple opponents.

In the beginning, the *Dágway* are followed as a pre-set sequence of movements and manoeuvres. However, as the practitioner gains competence in the strikes, blocks, footwork, and stances of the system, the *Dágway* themselves become a structure into which is inserted your own free-form expression. Thus, the *Dágway* become the basis of *Karenza* (improvisation) in the system.

In the images that follow for each of the *Dágway*, it should become clear how both the weapon hand and the alive hand are in constant coordinated motion; another signature of the system.

DÁGWAY-1

In *Dágway-1* you advance in one direction, executing all *12 Opensa* in sequence, then turn and advance in the opposite direction repeating your execution of the *12 Opensa*. Finish by turning and returning to your starting position.

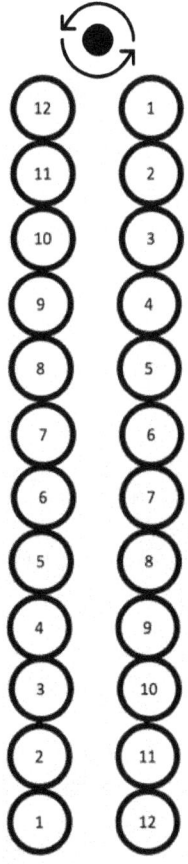

In the images that follow, we have tried to capture the dynamic movement of both the weapon and alive hands. They are constantly supporting or counterbalancing each other during the execution of the strikes.

We have used letter symbols to indicate the opening movements of each section of the form, and Roman numerals for the closing movements. The numbers used in-between represent each of the 12 Opensa.

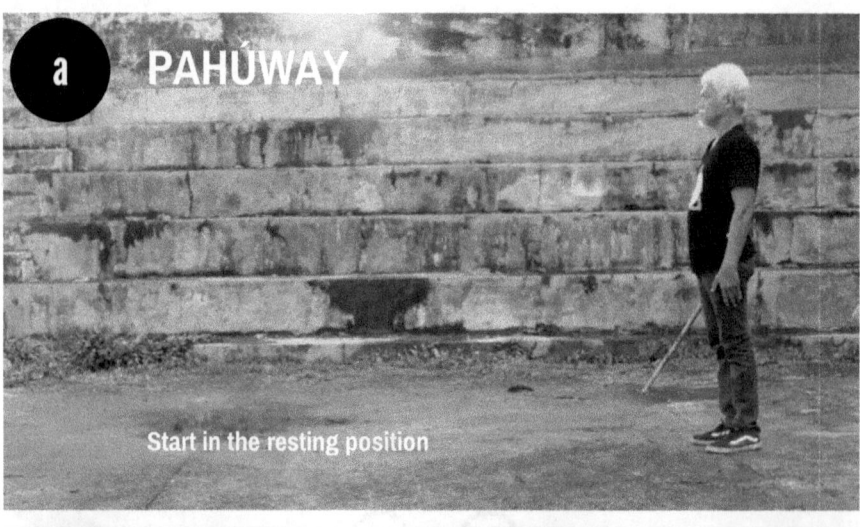

d. PIGAR & GARÁHE
Push with your alive hand while raising your weapon

1. OPENSA-1
Diagonal downwards *Tapás* forehand strike to temple

2. OPENSA-2
Diagonal downwards *Tapás* backhand strike to temple

3. OPENSA-3

Diagonal upwards *Hagbás* forehand strike to knees

Finish your strike in Kulob Serrada

4. OPENSA-4

Diagonal upwards *Hagbás* backhand strike to knees

Finish your strike in Kayà Abierta, then rotate your wrist into Kulob ready to thrust

5. OPENSA-5

***Kulob Totsada* (palm down thrust) to the chest**

Finish your strike in Kulob Serrada, then rotate your wrist into Kayà ready to thrust

6 OPENSA-6

Kayâ Totsada (pam up thrust) to chest

7 OPENSA-7

Vertical downward *Dagdag* strike to top of head

8 OPENSA-8

Straight *Totsada* thrust to torso

9 OPENSA-9
Horizontal backhand *Waslik* strike to ear or side of head

10 OPENSA-10
Horizontal forehand *Labô* strike to ear or side of head

11 OPENSA-11
Upward backhand *Witik* strike to groin

12 — OPENSA-12
Palm up *Totsada* thrust to eyes

i — PIVOT + PIGAR
Turn to your left pulling *Punyo* to chest and pushing with hand

ii — ARKO
Rotate the weapon downwards to your side

iii PAHÚWAY

Adopt the resting position

a PIGAR & GARÁHE

Step backward with left foot into a forward stance while pushing with your hand and chambering the stick

b PREPARAR

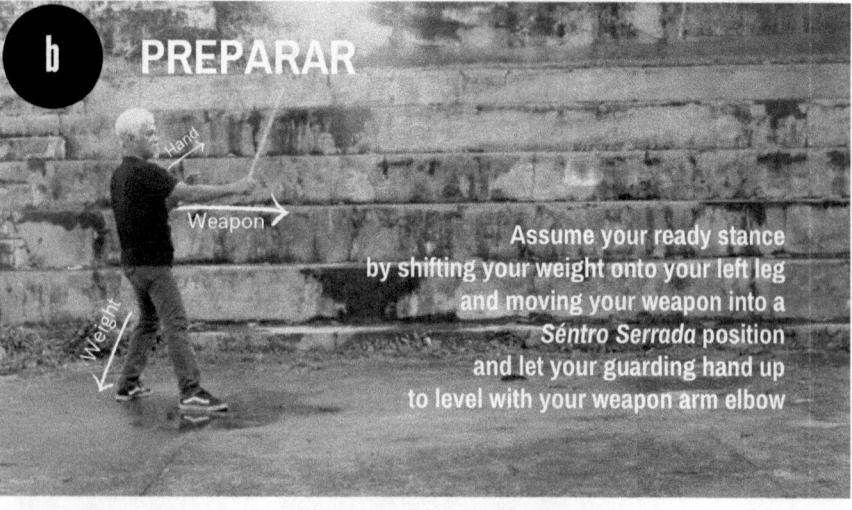

Assume your ready stance by shifting your weight onto your left leg and moving your weapon into a *Séntro Serrada* position and let your guarding hand up to level with your weapon arm elbow

C. PIGAR

Push with your alive hand as you step into Cat Stance and chamber your weapon over your right shoulder

1. OPENSA-1

Diagonal downwards *Tapás* forehand strike to temple

2. OPENSA-2

Diagonal downwards *Tapás* backhand strike to temple

3 OPENSA-3
Diagonal upwards *Hagbás* forehand strike to knees

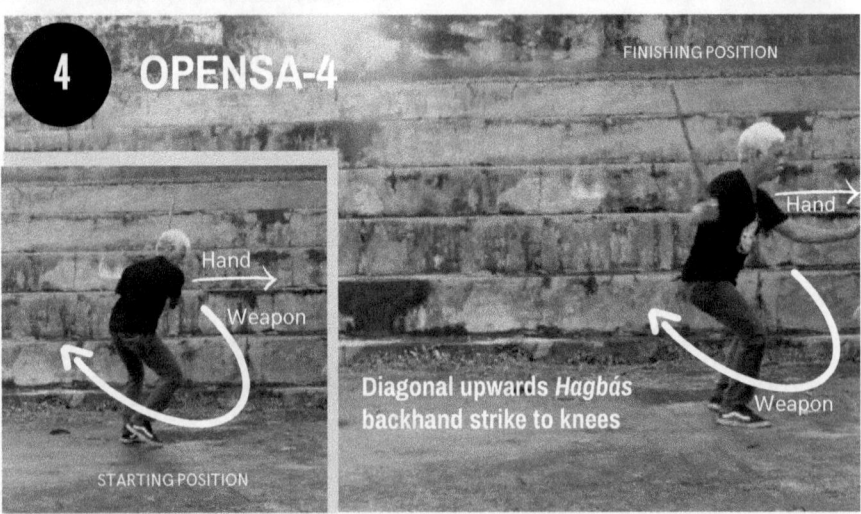

4 OPENSA-4
Diagonal upwards *Hagbás* backhand strike to knees

5 OPENSA-5
Kulob Totsada (pam down thrust) to the chest

OPENSA-6

Kayà Totsada (palm up thrust) to chest

OPENSA-7

Vertical downward *Dagdag* strike to top of head

OPENSA-8

Straight *Totsada* thrust to torso

12 OPENSA-12

Kayà Totsada (palm up thrust) to eyes

i PIVOT + PIGAR

Turn to your left, pulling punyo to chest, and pushing with alive hand

ii ARKO

Rotate the weapon downwards to your side

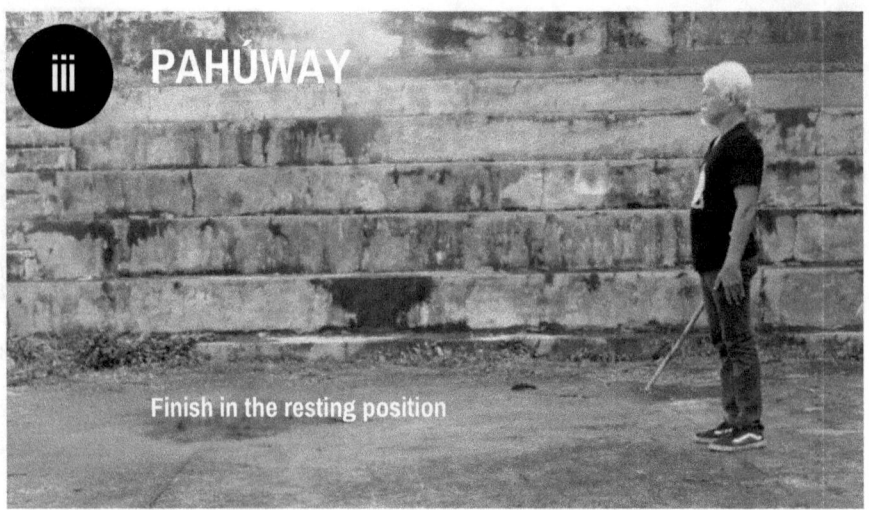

iii PAHÚWAY

Finish in the resting position

DÁGWAY-2

In *Dágway-2* you advance in one direction, executing all *12 Depensa* in sequence, then turn and advance in the opposite direction repeating your execution of the *12 Depensa*. Finish by turning and returning to your starting position.

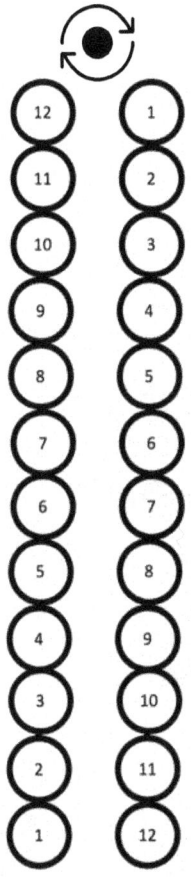

In the images that follow, we have tried to capture the dynamic movement of both the weapon and alive hands. They are constantly supporting each other during the execution of the *Depensa*.

We have used letter symbols to indicate the opening movements of each section of the form, and Roman numerals for the closing movements. The numbers used in-between represent each of the *12 Depensa*.

a PAHÚWAY

Start in resting position

b SALUDO

Bring your feet together
your weapon hand to your chest
with the tip pointing upwards
and bow to the front

c PREPARAR

Step backward with left foot
into a Back Stance
while extending your weapon
in a *Serrada Séntro* position
and your alive hand positioned
on the centreline of your torso

1. DEPENSA-1

Step diagonally forward to the right into a Forward Stance defending against a downward diagonal forehand strike aimed at your left temple

Meet the strike with your own diagonal forehand *De Pondo* block, shooting your *Pigar* (thumb down) over the top of your weapon arm

2. DEPENSA-2

Step diagonally forward to the left into a Forward Stance defending against a downward diagonal backhand strike aimed at your right temple

Meet the strike with your own diagonal backhand *De Pondo* block, following a parallel trajectory with your *Pigar* (thumb down)

3. DEPENSA-3

Step diagonally forward to the right into a Horse Stance defending against an upward diagonal forehand strike aimed at your knees

Meet the strike with your own downward forehand *De Pondo* block, shooting your *Pigar* (thumb down) over the top of your weapon arm

④ DEPENSA-4

Step diagonally forward to the left into a Forward Stance defending against an upward diagonal backhand strike aimed at your knees

Meet the strike with your own downward diagonal backhand *De Pondo* block, following a parallel trajectory with your *Pigar* (thumb up)

⑤ DEPENSA-5

Step diagonally forward to the right into a Forward Stance defending against a palm down thrust aimed at your chest

Deflect the strike with a *Páyong* (umbrella) block, shooting your *Pigar* (thumb up) underneath your weapon arm

⑥ DEPENSA-6

Step diagonally forward to the left into a Forward Stance defending against a palm up thrust aimed at your chest

Deflect the strike with a backhand *De Pondo* block, following a parallel trajectory with your *Pigar* (thumb up)

7. DEPENSA-7

Step diagonally forward to the right into a Forward Stance defending against a straight downward strike aimed at the top of your head

Deflect the strike with a backhand *Waslik* block, following a parallel trajectory with your *Pigar* (thumb down)

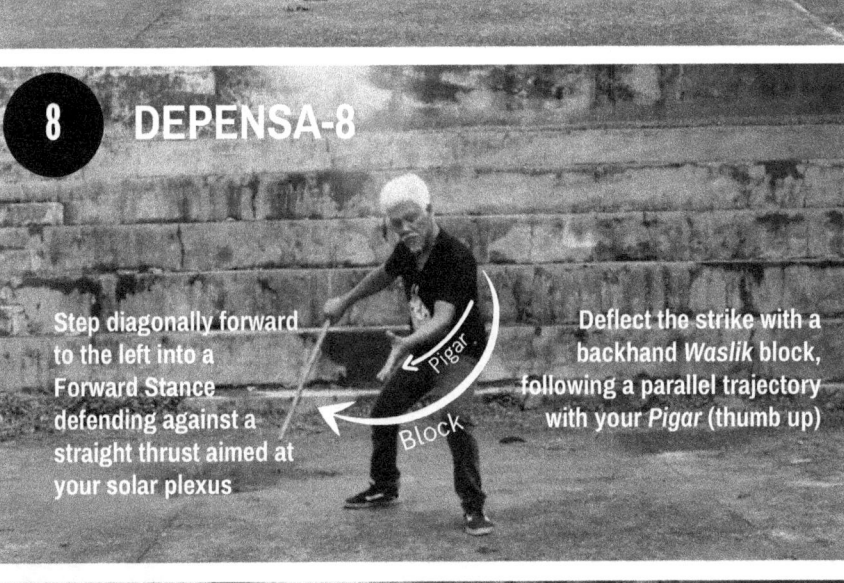

8. DEPENSA-8

Step diagonally forward to the left into a Forward Stance defending against a straight thrust aimed at your solar plexus

Deflect the strike with a backhand *Waslik* block, following a parallel trajectory with your *Pigar* (thumb up)

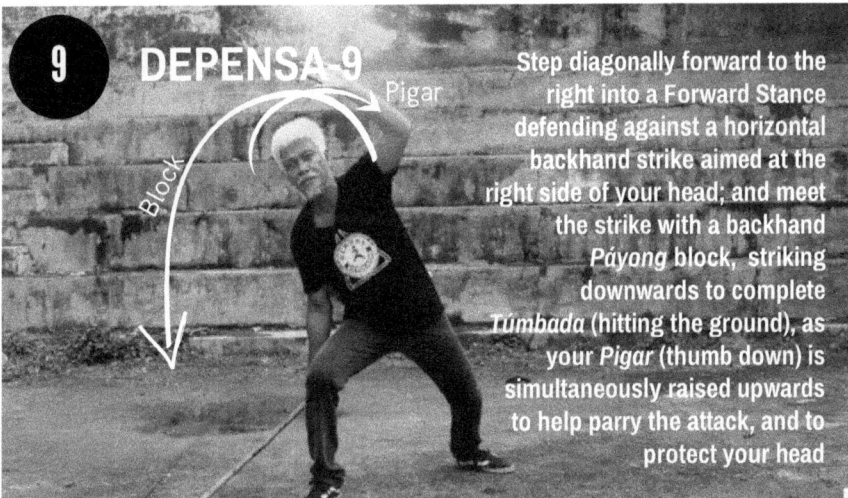

9. DEPENSA-9

Step diagonally forward to the right into a Forward Stance defending against a horizontal backhand strike aimed at the right side of your head; and meet the strike with a backhand *Páyang* block, striking downwards to complete *Túmbada* (hitting the ground), as your *Pigar* (thumb down) is simultaneously raised upwards to help parry the attack, and to protect your head

DEPENSA-10

Step diagonally forward to the left into a Forward Stance defending against a horizontal forehand strike aimed at the side of your head

Meet the strike with a forehand *De Pondo* block, shooting your *Pigar* (thumb down) over your weapon arm

DEPENSA-11

Step diagonally forward to the right into a Forward Stance defending against an upward backhand strike aimed at your groin

Meet the strike with a backhand *De Pondo* block, shooting your *Pigar* (thumb up) over your weapon arm

DEPENSA-12

Step diagonally forward to the left into a Forward Stance defending against a palm up thrust aimed at your face

Deflect the strike with a *Waslik* block, following a parallel trajectory with your *Pigar* (thumb down)

i. PIVOT + PIGAR
Turn to your left, pulling punyo to chest, and pushing with alive hand

ii. ARKO
Rotate the weapon downwards to your side

iii. PAHÚWAY
Finish in the resting position

a
PIGAR & GARÁHE
Pigar
Garáhe
Step backward with left foot
into a forward stance,
while pushing with your hand
and chambering the stick
Leg

b
PREPARAR
Weapon
Weight Shift
Shift your weight onto your
left leg into a Back Stance,
as you bring your weapon to
a *Séntro* position and your
hand into a guard position
near your elbow

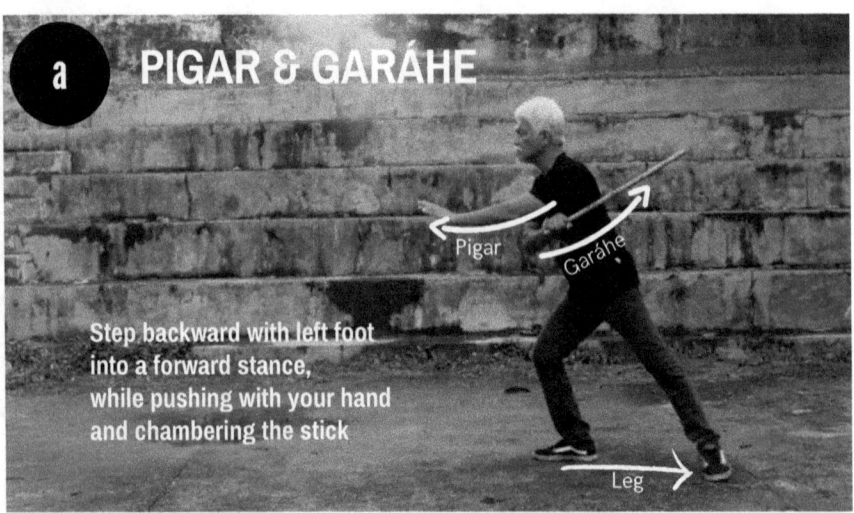

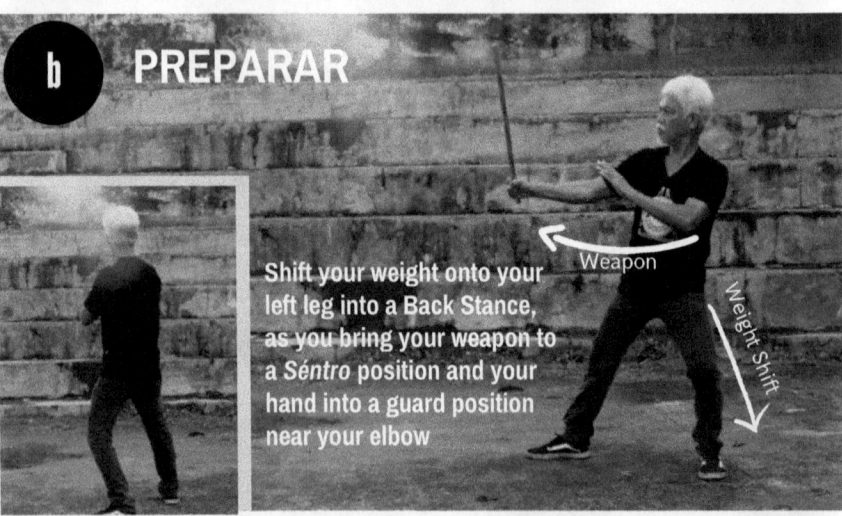

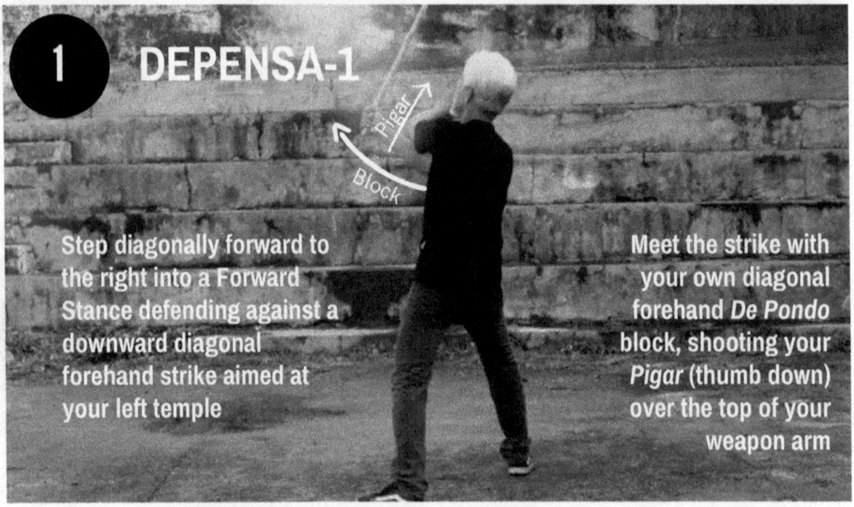

1
DEPENSA-1
Pigar
Block
Step diagonally forward to
the right into a Forward
Stance defending against a
downward diagonal
forehand strike aimed at
your left temple
Meet the strike with
your own diagonal
forehand *De Pondo*
block, shooting your
Pigar (thumb down)
over the top of your
weapon arm

2 · DEPENSA-2

Step diagonally forward to the left into a Forward Stance defending against a downward diagonal backhand strike aimed at your right temple

Meet the strike with your own diagonal backhand *De Pondo* block, following a parallel trajectory with your *Pigar* (thumb down)

3 · DEPENSA-3

Step diagonally forward to the right into a Horse Stance defending against an upward diagonal forehand strike aimed at your knees

Meet the strike with your own downward forehand *De Pondo* block, shooting your *Pigar* (thumb down) over the top of your weapon arm

4 · DEPENSA-4

Step diagonally forward to the left into a Forward Stance defending against an upward diagonal backhand strike aimed at your knees

Meet the strike with your own downward diagonal backhand *De Pondo* block, following a parallel trajectory with your *Pigar* (thumb up)

DEPENSA-5

Step diagonally forward to the right into a Forward Stance defending against a palm down thrust aimed at your chest

Deflect the strike with a *Páyong* (umbrella) block, shooting your *Pigar* (thumb up) underneath your weapon arm

DEPENSA-6

Step diagonally forward to the left into a Forward Stance defending against a palm up thrust aimed at your chest

Deflect the strike with a backhand *De Pondo* block, following a parallel trajectory with your *Pigar* (thumb up)

DEPENSA-7

Step diagonally forward to the right into a Forward Stance defending against a straight downward strike aimed at the top of your head

Deflect the strike with a backhand *Waslik* block, following a parallel trajectory with your *Pigar* (thumb down)

8. DEPENSA-8

Step diagonally forward to the left into a Forward Stance defending against a straight thrust aimed at your torso

Deflect the strike with a backhand *Waslik* block, following a parallel trajectory with your *Pigar* (thumb up)

9. DEPENSA-9

Step diagonally forward to the right into a Forward Stance defending against a horizontal backhand strike aimed at the right side of your head

Then meet the strike with a backhand *Payong* block, striking downwards to complete *Túmbada*, as your *Pigar* (thumb down) is simultaneously raised upwards to help sweep the attack off your *Páyong*, and to protect your head

10. DEPENSA-10

Step diagonally forward to the left into a Forward Stance defending against a horizontal forehand strike aimed at the side of your head

Meet the strike with a forehand *De Pondo* block, shooting your *Pigar* (thumb down) over your weapon arm

11 DEPENSA-11

Step diagonally forward to the right into a Forward Stance defending against an upward backhand strike aimed at your groin

Meet the strike with a backhand *De Pondo* block, shooting your *Pigar* (thumb up) over your weapon arm

12 DEPENSA-12

Step diagonally forward to the left into a Forward Stance defending against a palm up thrust aimed at your face

Deflect the strike with a *Waslik* block, following a parallel trajectory with your *Pigar* (thumb down)

i PIGAR

Pull the *Punyo* of your weapon towards your chest, as you pull back your right leg and pivot to face your starting direction, and *Pigar* in the direction you are facing with your alive hand

ii ARKO

Drop your alive hand to your left side as you rotate your weapon on your right side

iii PAHÚWAY

Completing the action by bringing both weapon and alive hand by your sides

iv PAHÚWAY

Step out with your left foot so that you stand at ease in *Pahúway* (the resting position)

DÁGWAY-3

Dágway-3 is built on a cross pattern. This is where you really begin to experience Bernas Estocadas' multi-directional movement, designed to build your skill in facing multiple opponents.

We recommend drawing the following numerical pattern on the floor of your training area. Each number represents one of the *Opensa*, and the arms of the cross represent the direction in which it should be executed for this *Dágway*. We have used compass directions to help you navigate the form. The larger of the two diagrams is the way you would see the numbers if facing North yourself. The smaller diagram is how the directions manifest if you are looking at the images of the *Dágway* on the following pages.

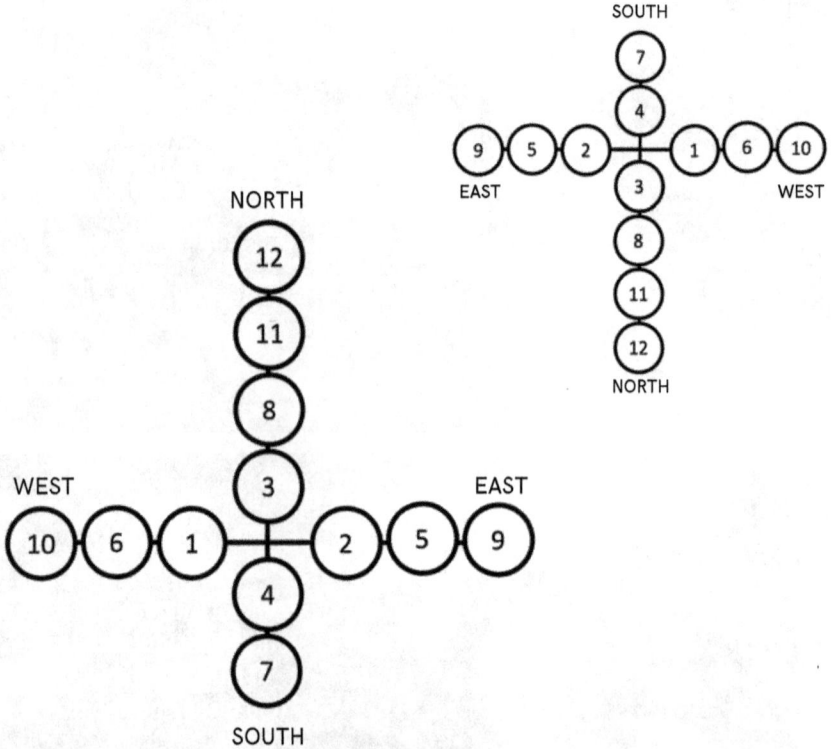

In the sequences that follow, we have used the ALPHA symbol for the opening section, and the OMEGA symbol for the closing section of the form. The heart of the form is based around the *12 Opensa*, and each section is identified by its associated number.

Start in *Pahúway* (the resting position), facing the North (in terms of how you have marked out the four directions in your training space)

Bring your feet together as you raise your weapon keeping the tip pointing upwards and your fist over your chest to start the *Saludo* (Salute)

Bow to complete the *Saludo*

Step back into *Preparar*

Draw your weapon back into chamber over your right shoulder as you step into Cat Stance, and *Pigar* with your alive hand

Turn to face an imaginary opponent coming at you from the West

Step to the West as you strike downwards with a diagonal forehand (Opensa 1) *Tapás* strike to your imaginary opponent's left temple

Complete your strike as you step into Cat Stance, with your weapon resting in the crook of your left arm

Turn to your right to face an imaginary opponent who has come from the East as you raise your weapon up over your left shoulder (high *Serrada* position)

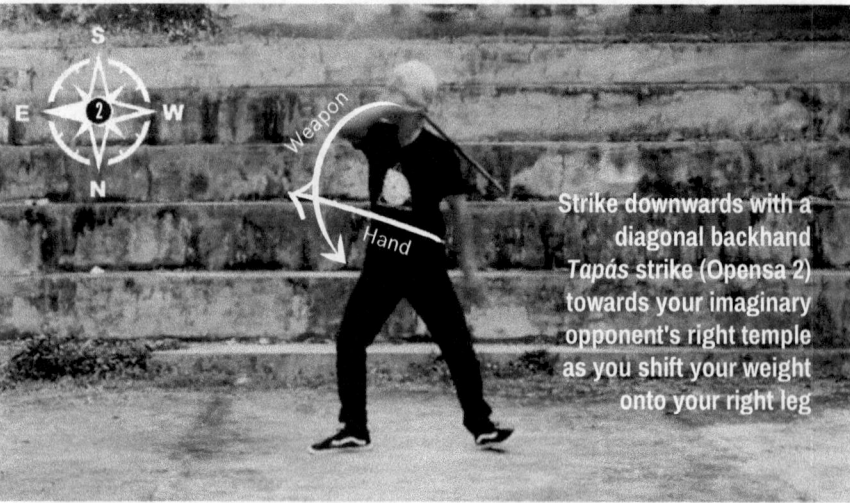

As you turn to face the North, swing your alive hand in a narrow arc to the rear (as if pulling an arm), as you step forward and scoop upwards with a forehand *Hagbás* strike (Opensa 3) to the opponent's knees

As your alive hand continues its arc, your weight shifts onto your front leg forming a Forward Stance as you continue to scoop upwards with your forehand *Hagbás* strike to the knees

Your alive hand terminates by your side and pointing slightly to the rear, while your stick completes its arc and terminates in a *Serrada* position resting in the crook of your left arm

Turn to face an opponent coming at you from the South

Step to the South and *Hágbas* by swinging your weapon in a scooping motion, striking towards your opponent's knees (Opensa 4), as your alive hand follows in a similar arc

As your weapon passes through the lowest point of its scooping arc and starts to rise, the alive hand pushes forward as a *Pigar*, as you shift into a Forward Stance

Complete your *Hagbás* strike by bringing your weapon into a high *Abierta* chamber while you execute *Pigar* with your alive hand, and finish in Cat Stance

Switch your wrist from *Kayâ* to *Kulob* so the point of your weapon points toward an opponent coming from the East

Step to the East as you begin a palm down *Totsada* (thrust) at the opponent's chest, using your alive hand to parry from your left to the right

Complete your *Totsada* to your opponent's chest in a Forward Stance, with your alive hand guarding the right side of your neck

Bring your weapon down to your side as you pivot to the West

Switch your wrist from *Kulob* to *Kayâ* so that the point of your weapon points toward an opponent coming from the West

Step to the West as you begin a palm up *Totsada* (thrust) at the opponent's chest, using your alive hand to parry from your the front to the back, like stroking a horse's main

Complete your *Totsada* to your opponent's chest in a Forward Stance, with your alive hand counterbalancing to your left rear

Turn to face an opponent coming from the South as you bring your trailing leg forward into a Cat Stance, and raise your weapon ready to strike

As you complete your Cat Stance, *Dagdag* (strike downward) to the opponent's head (Opensa 7) terminating as your stick executes a *Túmbada* (strike to the ground) beside your right leg, as your alive hand rises to protect your head

Spin to face an opponent coming from the North as you bring your alive hand down to your side, and start lifting your weapon for a thrust to the opponent's torso (Opensa 8)

Complete your spin and *Totsada* (thrust) in a Forward Stance facing the North

Step forward (still facing the North) with your left (rear) leg, as you bring your weapon across your body into a *Serrada* position

Turn to face an opponent coming from the East by shifting your weight onto your left leg and pivoting to your right

As you turn, parry from left to right, following your parry with a horizontal backhand *Waslik* strike towards your opponent's right ear

Complete your horizontal *Waslik* strike towards your opponent's right ear (Opensa 9), finishing in Cat Stance facing East

Turn to face an opponent coming from the West, by stepping to the North-East with your right leg, and starting to swing your alive hand to the West as you lift your weapon into a *Páyong* (umbrella) block

Continue turning to the West, by pivoting on your right foot, and swinging your weapon around into a horizontal forehand *Labô* strike to the opponent's left ear (Opensa 10), while sweeping your alive hand down to your left side

Finishing facing the West in a Cat Stance with your weight on your right foot, as you complete your horizontal forehand *Labô* strike to the opponent's left ear (Opensa 10)

Step to the South with your left foot as you chamber your weapon over your left shoulder

Facing an opponent from the North, shift your weight onto your left leg forming a Back Stance, as you parry across your body underneath your weapon arm with your alive hand, and start to swing your weapon in a half-circle to the North

Staying in the Back Stance, complete the arc of your weapon so it now swings upward into the opponent's groin (Opensa 11) with your alive hand protecting your ribs

As you alive hand continues in its arc upwards to the rear, and your weight starts to shift onto your front leg

Complete the circle of your weapon so the point starts to face South, and then completes the arc to face the North

Complete your *Totsada* (thrust) to the opponent's eyes as you enter into a Forward Stance, and counterbalance the movement with your alive hand extended to the rear

Pull the *punyo* of your weapon towards your heart, as you pull back your right leg, and *Pigar* in the direction you are facing (North) with your alive hand

Drop your alive hand to your left side as you rotate your weapon on your right side

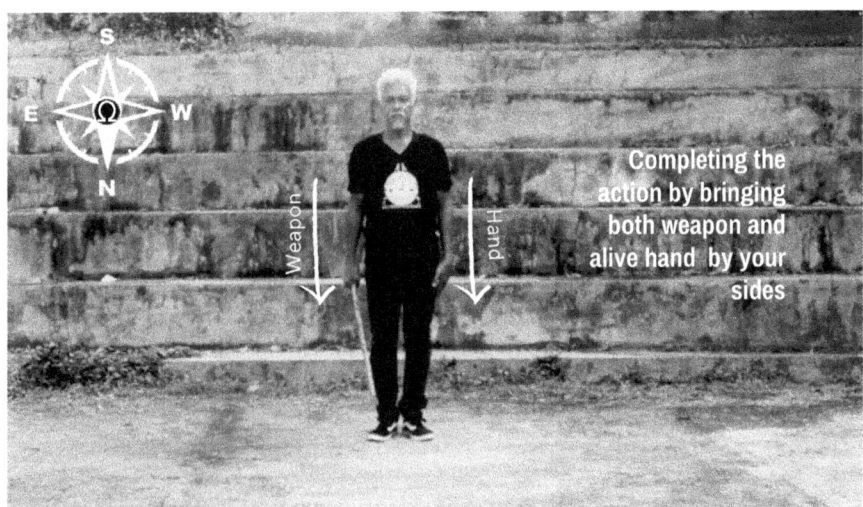

Completing the action by bringing both weapon and alive hand by your sides

Step out with your left foot so that you stand at ease in *Pahúway* (the resting position)

DÁGWAY-4

Dágway-4 is, like *Dágway-3,* built on a cross pattern, and is where you really begin to experience Bernas Estocadas' multi-directional movement, designed to build your skill in facing multiple opponents.

We recommend drawing the following numerical pattern on the floor of your training area. Each number represents one of the *Depensa,* and the arms of the cross represent the direction in which it should be executed for this *Dágway.* We have used compass directions to help you navigate the form. The larger of the two diagrams is the way you would see the numbers if facing North yourself. The smaller diagram is how the directions manifest if you are looking at the images of the *Dágway* on the following pages.

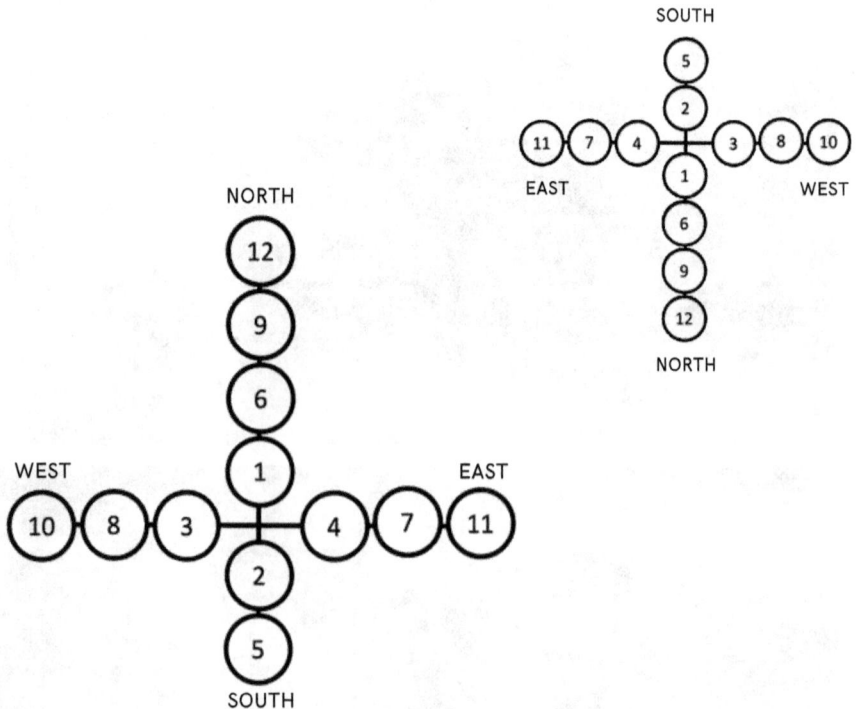

In the sequences that follow, we have used the ALPHA symbol for the opening section, and the OMEGA symbol for the closing section of the form. The heart of the form is based around the *12 Opensa,* and each section is identified by its associated number.

Start in *Pahúway* (the resting position), facing the North (in terms of how you have marked out the four directions in your training space)

Bring your feet together as you raise your weapon keeping the tip pointing upwards and your fist over your chest to start the *Saludo* (Salute)

Bow to complete the *Saludo*

Step back into *Preparar*

As you step forward to meet a downward diagonal forehand strike aimed at your head (Opensa 1), draw your weapon back and aim your *Punyo* towards the direction of the imagined attack

As you shift into a Forward Stance, snap your weapon forward with your own diagonal forehand *De Pondo* block (Depensa 1) to meet the imagined Opensa 1 attack; Your *Pigar* (thumb down) should come in over your weapon arm as you execute the block

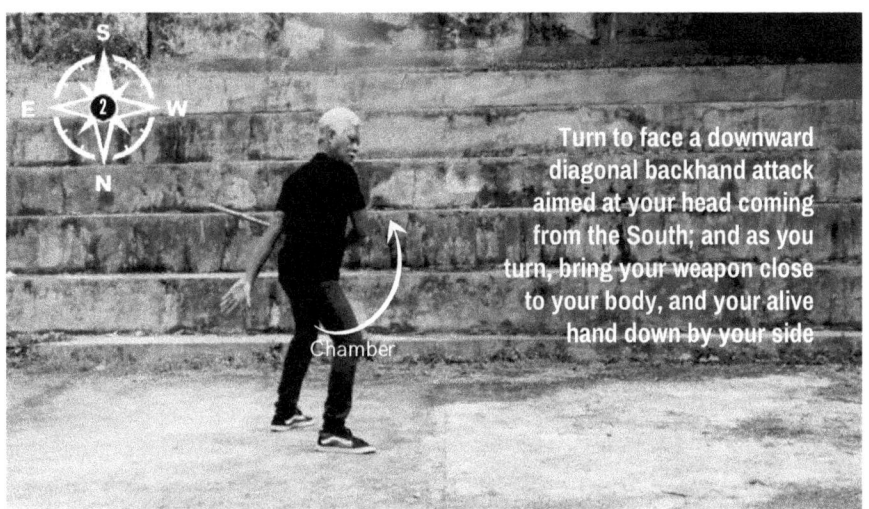

Turn to face a downward diagonal backhand attack aimed at your head coming from the South; and as you turn, bring your weapon close to your body, and your alive hand down by your side

The snap your weapon out to with your own diagonal backhand *De Pondo* block (Depensa 2), knocking away an imagined Opensa 2 attack. Your *Pigar* (thumb down) follows a parallel trajectory to your weapon as you execute the block

Turn to face an upward diagonal forehand strike aimed at your knees coming from the West; and as you turn, chamber your weapon over your right shoulder

As you step into Horse Stance, slam your weapon down against an imagined Opensa 3 attack with a Depensa 3 *De Pondo* style block; Your *Pigar* (thumb down) should come in over your weapon arm as you execute the block

Turn to face an upward diagonal backhand strike aimed at your knees coming from the East; and as you turn, chamber your weapon over your left shoulder, with your alive hand by your left side

As you shift into a Forward Stance, swing your weapon down against an imagined Opensa 4 attack with a Depensa 4 *De Pondo* style block. Your *pigar* (thumb up) follows a parallel trajectory to your weapon as you execute the block

5 — Turn to face a palm down thrust aimed at your chest coming from the South; and as you turn, immediately lift your weapon into a *Páyong* (umbrella) position, deflecting the Opensa 5 thrust off-course with your Depensa 5 block

Shoot your *Pigar* (thumb up) in underneath your weapon just after your deflection of the attack

6 — Turn to face a palm up thrust aimed at your chest coming from the North; and as you turn, chamber your weapon over your left arm (forming a *Serrada* position), with your alive hand by your left side

6 — As you shift into a Forward Stance, swing your weapon at a slightly diagonal angle against an imagined Opensa 6 attack with a Depensa 6 *De Pondo* style block

Your *Pigar* (thumb down) follows a parallel trajectory to your weapon as you execute the block

7 Turn to face a strike coming straight down at your head from the East; and as you turn, bring your weapon across your torso (forming a *Kulob Serrada* position), with your alive hand by your left side

Chamber

Block

7 As you step into a Forward Stance, deflect an imagined Opensa 7 attack with a Depensa 7 *Waslik* style block

Pigar

Your *Pigar* (thumb down) follows an almost parallel trajectory to your weapon, pushing forward as the block is executed

8 Turn to face a straight thrust aimed at your midsection coming from the West; and as you turn, bring your weapon across your torso (forming a *Kulob Serrada* position), with your alive hand by your left side

Chamber

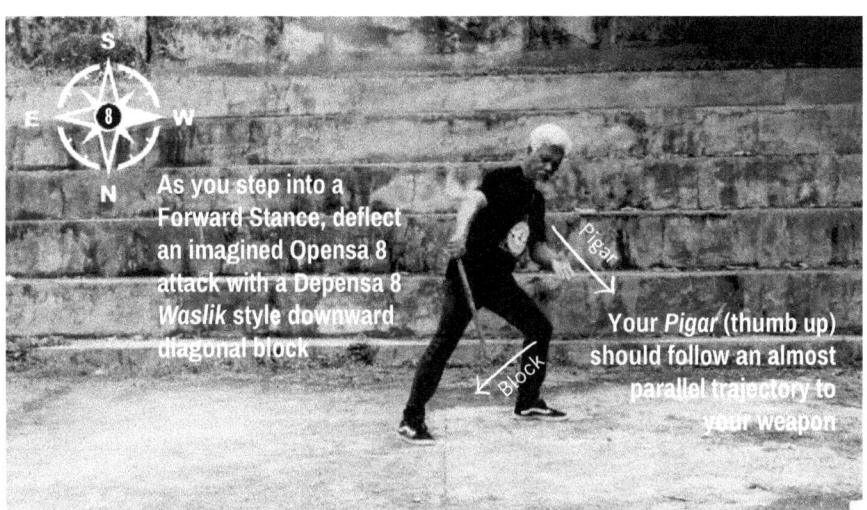

As you step into a Forward Stance, deflect an imagined Opensa 8 attack with a Depensa 8 *Waslik* style downward diagonal block

Your *Pigar* (thumb up) should follow an almost parallel trajectory to your weapon

Turn to face a horizontal strike aimed at your right ear, coming from the North

As you turn, chamber your weapon over your left shoulder, with your alive hand by your left side

As you step into a Forward Stance, you duck and meet your imagined opponent's Opensa 9 attack with a *Páyong* (umbrella) performed as a *Derecho* strike and passing the opponent's weapon with your alive hand as you *Túmbada* (forcefully strike the ground)

Turn to face an Opensa 10 horizontal strike aimed at your left ear, coming from the West; and as you turn, immediately strike the opponent's weapon with your own De Pondo style tip-up forehand block

Your *Pigar* (thumb down) shoots in over your arm as the block is executed

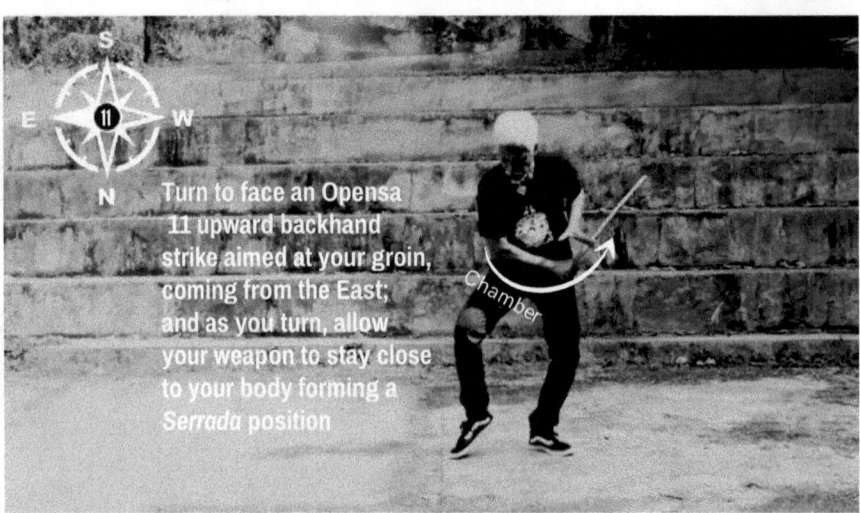

Turn to face an Opensa 11 upward backhand strike aimed at your groin, coming from the East; and as you turn, allow your weapon to stay close to your body forming a *Serrada* position

As you step into a Forward Stance, meet the opponent's Opensa 11 attack with your own backhand *De Pondo* block, shooting your *pigar* (thumb down) in above your weapon arm

Turn to face an Opensa 12 palm up thrust to your face coming from the North; and as you turn, allow your weapon to stay close to your body (forming a *Serrada* position), with your alive hand by your left side

As you step into a Forward Stance, deflect the opponent's Opensa 12 attack with a backhand *Waslik* strike, allowing your *pigar* (thumb down) to shoot out as you execute the block

Pull the *Punyo* of your weapon towards your heart, as you pull back your left leg, and *Pigar* in the direction you are facing (North) with your *Ngangáng Buáya* (crocodile mouth or alive hand)

8

OPENSA-DEPENSA
ATTACK & DEFENCE

OPENSA-DEPENSA

The *Opensa-Depensa* (Attack-Defence) drill is the foundational combative partner drill in the Bernas Estocadas system. This drill has its analogue in the block-check-counter drills of other Filipino Martial Art systems. However, a special emphasis in *Opensa-Depensa* is to develop the capacity to defend against impact or edged weapons, and it is in its to-and-fro, high-and-low, countering patterns that the influence of *Wedo* is truly registered.

The Opensa-Depensa drill is initially practiced with *Bastón* (sticks). However, as the practitioner's skill increases, the drill can be practiced with a blunt training *Talibóng* (sword) so the proper angles can be fine-tuned. To assist with learning from the images, and to demonstrate the translation of the *Bastón* (stick) techniques to the blade, the following demonstration of the *Opensa-Depensa* is performed with blunted *Talibóng* (swords). Of course, we recommend starting with rattan sticks, and moving to wooden or polyurethane training swords, and seeking direct instruction from a qualified teacher before moving to blunt metal weapons.

CORRECT FEEDING AND STAGES OF PRACTICE

Stage 1 De Pondo: When you first start practicing this drill, the feeder should execute all their attacks in *De Pondo* (anchored) fashion. This means that each attack stops at (or just before) the target, rather than penetrating it; and will be devoid of any follow through motion. This allows the defender to develop proper technique, without the pressure of getting hit if they execute a block incorrectly.

Stage 2 Derecho: Later, as the practitioner's skill develops, attacks may be delivered in a more naturalistic *Derecho* (direct) fashion, with a fluid follow through. Even when executed in this fashion, the feeder should be responsible with their technique, and be ready to abort the attack if the defender executes an incorrect or ineffective defence.

Stage 3 Hánas: Once both feeder and defender have a good level of skill in their execution of the techniques, additional pressure-testing can occur by practicing the drill wearing protective head gear and using padded sticks. Here the feeder will actually try to make contact with the target, so the defender really must work their blocks and counters.

THREE FUNDAMENTAL LEVELS OF OPENSA-DEPENSA

In addition to the training stages described above, the *Opensa-Depensa* drill platform has a number of levels (each represented by their associated start and end key in the sequences that follow):

Level 1 | Blocking
In the first level of the *Opensa-Depensa* drill, the feeder attacks with the first *Opensa*, and the defender meets the attack with the appropriate paired *Depensa*. This is repeated eight times. The feeder then moves on to the next *Opensa* in sequence, until the defender has practiced blocking against all *12 Opensa*. Once the defender is comfortable defending against all *12 Opensa*, the feeder may attack out of sequence, and at irregular intervals, to add additional pressure to the drill.

Level 2 | Counters
In the second level of the *Opensa-Depensa* drill, the feeder again attacks with the first *Opensa*, and the defender meets the attack with the appropriate paired *Depensa*, then applying their *Pigar* (pressure) to the opponent's weapon hand, pushes it out of the way to clear a path for a single counterstrike, which they then execute. This is repeated eight times. The feeder then moves on to the next *Opensa* in sequence, until the defender has practiced blocking and countering against all *12 Opensa*. Once again, when the defender is comfortable defending against all *12 Opensa*, the feeder may attack out of sequence, and at irregular intervals, to add additional pressure to the drill.

Level 3 | Multiple Counters
In the third level of the *Opensa-Depensa* drill, the feeder again attacks with the first *Opensa*, and the defender meets the attack with the appropriate paired *Depensa*, then applying their *Pigar* (pressure) to the opponent's weapon hand, pushes it out of the way to clear a path for their multiple counterstrikes, which they then execute. This is repeated eight times. The feeder then moves on to the next *Opensa* in sequence, until the defender has practiced blocking and multiple counters against all *12 Opensa*. Once again, when the defender is comfortable defending against all *12 Opensa*, the feeder may attack out of sequence, and at irregular intervals, to add additional pressure to the drill.

A NOTE ABOUT MULTIPLE COUNTER PATTERNS

A key principle in the Bernas Estocadas system is to change the elevation of your strikes, to disrupt the opponent's ability to counter, and to make you a moving target. This principle is built into the multiple counters drill, and is outlined in the table below (where the attacks are listed by their name, and the counterattack combination is listed as a set of numbers). This table reveals that 1-2-3 is the most common counterattack pattern, followed by 2-1-4, with a different pattern for *Opensa-Depensa 4 & 8*, and unique patterns for *Opensa-Depensa 10 & 11*. Because the majority of attacks are to high targets, the most common counters move from high to low.

High-Low			Low-High
1-2-3	**2-1-4**	**2-3-4-3**	**3-9-10**
Opensa 2 Opensa 6 Opensa 7 Opensa 9 Opensa 12	Opensa 1 Opensa 3 Opensa 5	Opensa 11	Opensa 4 Opensa 8
1-2-3-4			
Opensa 10			

THREE ADVANCED LEVELS OF OPENSA-DEPENSA

There are three additional, more advanced levels, we hope to cover in a future volume on the *Pang-Áway* (Combatives) of Bernas Estocadas:

Level 4 | Evasion
During the execution of the Level 3 Multiple Counters, a second attack is thrown by the feeder, which the defender must evade and parry, as they continue their counters.

Level 5 | Disarms
After the Level 1 Blocking defence, the defender immediately applies a disarm, snatching or ejecting the opponent's weapon from their grasp.

Level 6 | Disarms with Multiple Counters
After applying the Level 5 Disarm, the defender immediately follows up with multiple counterstrikes.

OPENSA-DEPENSA

LEVEL 1 BLOCKING | Depensa 1

The feeder attacks with *Opensa 1* and the defender executes *Depensa 1* in response. Start in *Preparar* (Fig. 1). Feeder takes a short step with their right foot facilitating the chambering of their weapon over their right shoulder in a high *Abierta* position, as they press forward with their left hand (Fig. 2)., their left foot sliding up to meet the right foot as defender brings their weapon off the centreline, *Punyo* facing the opponent (Fig. 3). The feeder then steps diagonally forward with their left foot as they execute their *Tapás* (tree-felling) *Opensa 1* downward diagonal forehand strike towards the defender's head, while the defender starts to step offline diagonally forward to the right, raising their weapon to meet the attack (Fig. 4). The defender then intercepts the attack, striking it simultaneously downward and to the side, and bringing their alive hand over their weapon arm to capture the opponent's hand with their *Ngangáng Buáya* (crocodile mouth), completing the motion in a forward stance (Fig. 5).

LEVEL 2 COUNTER | Depensa 1 > Opensa 2

The defence against *Opensa 1* (Fig. 1-5) described above, is followed up by *Pigar* to the opponent's weapon hand, pushing it away and down, allowing the defender's weapon to naturally chamber behind their left shoulder (Fig. 6), and making space for the execution of a *Opensa 2* downward diagonal backhand counter (Fig. 7), terminating in an *Abierta* position (Fig. 8).

LEVEL 3 MULTIPLE COUNTERS | Depensa 1 > Opensa 2, 1, 4

The defence against *Opensa 1* (Fig. 1-5) described above, is followed up the *Opensa 2* counter (Fig. 6-8). Then the defender raises their weapon out to their right side, above the level of their right shoulder (Fig. 9), and cuts with an *Opensa 1* downward diagonal forehand counter (Fig. 10), as they shift their weight into a left-leaning forward stance (Fig. 11). With their weapon now in a low *Serrada* position, they step to the right (Fig. 12), and as they shift their weight onto their right foot, execute an *Opensa 4* upward diagonal backhand counter, cutting towards the feeder's lead-leg knee (Fig. 13), terminating in a low right-leaning forward stance with the weapon in an *Abierta* position (Fig. 14).

ALL LEVELS START HERE

END LEVEL 1 BLOCKING

OPENSA 2 COUNTER

END LEVEL 2 COUNTER

OPENSA 1 COUNTER

OPENSA 4 COUNTER

END LEVEL 3 MULTIPLE COUNTERS

OPENSA-DEPENSA

● 2

LEVEL 1 BLOCKING | Depensa 2

The feeder attacks with *Opensa 2* and the defender executes *Depensa 2* in response. Start in *Preparar* (Fig. 1). Feeder takes a short step with their right foot as they bring their weapon across their body into a *Serrada* position (Fig. 2)., their left foot sliding up to meet the right foot as they raise their weapon over their left shoulder; as defender starts to step left, bringing their weapon off the centreline, *Punyo* facing the opponent (Fig. 3). The feeder then steps diagonally forward with their left foot as they execute their *Tapás* (tree-felling) *Opensa 2* downward diagonal backhand strike towards the defender's head, while the defender starts to step offline diagonally forward to the left, raising their weapon and alive hand to meet the attack (Fig. 4).The defender then intercepts the attack with their own backhand block, striking the opponent's weapon downward and to the side, as they bring their alive hand up to capture the opponent's hand with their *Ngangáng Buáya* (crocodile mouth), completing the motion in a forward stance (Fig. 5).

LEVEL 2 COUNTER | Depensa 2 > Opensa 1

The defence against *Opensa 2* (Fig. 1-5) described above, is followed up by *Pigar* to the opponent's weapon hand, pushing it away and down (Fig. 6), allowing the defender's weapon to naturally chamber out to their right side at the level of the shoulder (Fig. 7), and making space for the execution of a *Opensa 1* downward diagonal forehand counter (Fig. 8), terminating in a *Serrada* position (Fig. 9).

LEVEL 3 MULTIPLE COUNTERS | Depensa 2 > Opensa 1, 2, 3

The defence against *Opensa 2* (Fig. 1-5) described above, is followed up the *Opensa 1* counter (Fig. 6-9). Then the defender raises their weapon above the level of their left shoulder in a *Serrada* position (Fig. 10), and cuts with an *Opensa 2* downward diagonal backhand counter (Fig. 11), as they shift their weight into a right-leaning forward stance (Fig. 12). Flipping their weapon hand from *Kulob* (palm down) to *Kayâ* (palm up), and with their weapon now in a low *Abierta* position, they use their alive hand to counterbalance (Fig. 13), as they shift their weight onto their left foot, executing an *Opensa 3* upward diagonal forehand counter, cutting towards the feeder's lead-leg knee (Fig. 14), terminating in a low left-leaning forward stance with the weapon in an *Serrada* position (Fig. 15).

ALL LEVELS START HERE

END LEVEL 1 BLOCKING — TRANSITION

BERNAS ESTOCADAS

OPENSA 1 COUNTER

END LEVEL 2 COUNTER

OPENSA 2 COUNTER

OPENSA 3 COUNTER

END LEVEL 3 MULTIPLE COUNTERS

OPENSA-DEPENSA

3

LEVEL 1 BLOCKING | Depensa 3

The feeder attacks with *Opensa 3* and the defender executes *Depensa 3* in response. Start in *Preparar* (Fig. 1). Feeder shifts their weight onto their right leg as they shift their weapon off the centreline to their right side (Fig. 2)., and as they start to step diagonally forward to the left with their left foot, the defender starts to raise their weapon with *Punyo* facing the opponent (Fig. 3). As the feeder completes their step diagonally forward with their left foot, they execute their *Hágbas* (grass-cutting) *Opensa 3* upward diagonal forehand attack towards the defender's leg, while the defender starts to step offline diagonally forward to the right, bringing their weapon down to meet the attack (Fig. 4). As the defender intercepts the attack, striking it downward, they simultaneously bring their alive hand over the opponent's weapon hand, applying their *Pigar*, as they complete the motion in a horse stance (Fig. 5).

LEVEL 2 COUNTER | Depensa 3 > Opensa 2

The defence against *Opensa 3* (Fig. 1-5) described above, is followed up by *Pigar* to the opponent's weapon hand, pushing it downward (Fig. 6), allowing the defender to raise their weapon beside their left shoulder as they shift their weight to the right (Fig. 7), making space for the execution of a *Opensa 2* downward diagonal backhand counter (Fig. 8).

LEVEL 3 MULTIPLE COUNTERS | Depensa 3 > Opensa 2, 1, 4

The defence against *Opensa 1* (Fig. 1-5) described above, is followed up the *Opensa 2* counter (Fig. 6-8). Then the defender raises their weapon out to their right side, as they start to step to the left (Fig. 9), and cuts with an *Opensa 1* downward diagonal forehand counter (Fig. 10), as they shift their weight into a left-leaning forward stance (Fig. 11). Flipping their wrist so that their weapon is now in a low Serrada position, they step to the right (Fig. 12), and as they shift their weight onto their right foot, execute an *Opensa 4* counter strike, cutting towards the feeder's lead leg with an upward diagonal backhand attack, checking the opponent's weapon hand with their *Pigar* (Fig. 13), as they terminate their counter in a low right-leaning forward stance with the weapon in an *Abierta* position (Fig. 14).

BERNAS ESTOCADAS

ALL LEVELS START HERE

END LEVEL 1 BLOCKING

BERNAS ESTOCADAS

OPENSA 2 COUNTER

END LEVEL 2 COUNTER

OPENSA 1 COUNTER

OPENSA 4 COUNTER

END LEVEL 3 MULTIPLE COUNTERS

OPENSA-DEPENSA

LEVEL 1 BLOCKING | Depensa 4

The feeder attacks with *Opensa 4* and the defender executes *Depensa 4* in response. Start in *Preparar* (Fig. 1). Feeder starts to lower their centre of mass as they bring their weapon across their chest (Fig. 2)., then as they step diagonally forward to the right they begin their *Hágbas* (grass-cutting) *Opensa 4* upward slash of their weapon, while the defender starts to lower their weapon and remove their lead leg from the line of the attack (Fig. 3). As the feeder completes their step, and starts to angle their weapon upwards towards the defender's leg, the defender removes their lead leg, and positions their weapon to meet the opponent's attack while reaching out with their *Ngangáng Buáya* (crocodile mouth) towards the opponent's weapon hand (Fig. 4).The defender then intercepts the attack, striking it to the side, while capturing the opponent's hand with their *Ngangáng Buáya*, as they complete the motion while maintaining a forward stance (Fig. 5).

LEVEL 2 COUNTER | Depensa 4 > Opensa 3

The defence against *Opensa 4* (Fig. 1-5) described above, is followed up by *Pigar* to the opponent's weapon hand, pushing it upwards and inwards (Fig. 6), as the defender flips or circles their hand into a *Kayâ* (palm up) position and begins to step forward with their right leg (Fig. 7). As they complete their weight shift onto the right leg, the defender executes an *Opensa 3* upward diagonal counter to the opoonent's leg (Fig. 8), completing their action in a high *Serrada* position (Fig. 9).

LEVEL 3 MULTIPLE COUNTERS | Depensa 4 > Opensa 3, 9, 10

The defence against *Opensa 4* (Fig. 1-5) described above, is followed up with the *Opensa 3* counter (Fig. 6-9). Flipping into a *Kulob* (palm down) position, and with their weapon raised in a high *Serrada* position over their left shoulder (Fig. 10), the defender begins turning to the right (Fig. 11), as they step to the side of their opponent with their left leg, executing an *Opensa 9* horizontal counter to the side of the opponent's head, and applying a *Pigar* to the opponent's weapon arm to prevent a counterattack (Fig. 12). Maintaining the *Pigar*, the defender raises their weapon above their head as if applying a *Payong* (umbrella block), while stepping to the right with their right leg (Fig. 13), and pivoting on their right leg, executes an *Opensa 10* horizontal counter to the opponent's neck (Fig. 14), stepping back with their left foot to form a forward stance, as they complete the counter (Fig. 15).

BERNAS ESTOCADAS

ALL LEVELS START HERE

END LEVEL 1 BLOCKING

TRANSITION

OPENSA 3 COUNTER

END LEVEL 2 COUNTER

OPENSA-DEPENSA

LEVEL 1 BLOCKING

The feeder attacks with *Opensa 5* and the defender executes *Depensa 5* in response. Start in *Preparar* (Fig. 1). Feeder shifts their weight onto their right leg as they draw their weapon so that the point of their weapon aims at the opponent's chest (Fig. 2). As the attacker steps to the left with their leg leg, they start to execute a *Kulob* (palm down) *Totsada* (thrust) at the opponent's chest, while the defender begins to step offline to the right with their right leg and starts to bring their weapon into a *Payong* (umbrella block) position (Fig. 3). As the attacker completes their thrust the defender meets the opponent's weapon with their *Payong*, deflecting it to the side (Fig. 4), and reaching underneath their own weapon arm with their alive hand (thumb upwards), applies their *Ngangáng Buáya* (crocodile mouth), as they complete the motion in a forward stance (Fig. 5).

LEVEL 2 COUNTER

The defence against *Opensa 5* (Fig. 1-5) described above, is followed up by *Pigar* to the opponent's weapon hand, pushing it away and to the side, as they rotate their weapon so it is ready to strike or cut downwards (Fig. 6). Then shifting more of their weight onto their right leg, the defender counters with an *Opensa 2* downward diagonal backhand attack (Fig. 7), maintaining their *Pigar* as they terminate their counter in a low *Abierta* position (Fig. 8).

LEVEL 3 MULTIPLE COUNTERS

The defence against *Opensa 5* (Fig. 1-5) described above, is followed up the *Opensa 2* counter (Fig. 6-8). Then the defender raises their weapon out to their right side, above the level of their right shoulder (Fig. 9), and cuts with an *Opensa 1* downward diagonal forehand counter (Fig. 10), as they shift their weight into a left-leaning forward stance (Fig. 11). Circling or flipping their weapon into a low *Serrada* position, they step to the right (Fig. 12), and as they shift their weight onto their right foot, execute an *Opensa 4* upward diagonal backhand counter strike, cutting towards the feeder's lead-leg (Fig. 13), terminating in a low right-leaning forward stance with the weapon in an *Abierta* position (Fig. 14).

ALL LEVELS START HERE

END LEVEL 1 BLOCKING

OPENSA 2 COUNTER

END LEVEL 2 COUNTER

OPENSA 1 COUNTER

OPENSA 4 COUNTER

END LEVEL 3 MULTIPLE COUNTERS

OPENSA-DEPENSA

LEVEL 1 BLOCKING | Depensa 6

The feeder attacks with *Opensa 6* and the defender executes *Depensa 6* in response. Start in *Preparar* (Fig. 1). Feeder sinks their weight as they bring their weapon across their body into a *Kayâ* (palm up) *Serrada* (closed) position aiming the point of their weapon at the defender's chest (Fig. 2). As they step forward with their right foot and commence their *Kayâ* (palm up) *Totsada* (thrust) the defender starts to offline by stepping to the left and turning their hand so that the edge of their weapon (if a sword) faces the incoming weapon (Fig. 3). The feeder then steps diagonally forward with their left foot as they meet the opponent's weapon with their own (Fig. 4). Intercepting the attack and deflecting the weapon to the side, the defender applies a Pigar to the opponent's forearm, and completes the motion in a left-side forward stance (Fig. 5).

LEVEL 2 COUNTER | Depensa 6 > Opensa 1

The defence against *Opensa 2* (Fig. 1-5) described above, is followed up by *pigar* to the opponent's weapon hand, pushing it away and down, allowing the defender's weapon to naturally chamber out to their right side at the level of the shoulder (Fig. 6), and making space for the execution of a *Opensa 1* downward diagonal forehand counter (Fig. 7), terminating in a *Serrada* position (Fig. 8).

LEVEL 3 MULTIPLE COUNTERS | Depensa 6 > Opensa 1, 2, 3

The defence against *Opensa 2* (Fig. 1-5) described above, is followed up the *Opensa 1* counter (Fig. 6-8). Then the defender raises their weapon above the level of their left shoulder in a *Serrada* position (Fig. 9), and executes an *Opensa 2* downward diagonal backhand counter (Fig. 10), as they shift their weight into a right-leaning forward stance (Fig. 11). Flipping their weapon hand from *Kulob* (palm down) to *Kayâ* (palm up), and with their weapon now in a low *Abierta* position, they use their alive hand to counterbalance (Fig. 12), as they shift their weight onto their left foot, executing an *Opensa 3* upward diagonal forehand counter, cutting towards the feeder's lead-leg knee (Fig. 13), terminating in a low left-leaning forward stance with the weapon in an *Serrada* position (Fig. 14).

ALL LEVELS START HERE

END LEVEL 1 BLOCKING

OPENSA 1 COUNTER

END LEVEL 2 COUNTER

OPENSA 2 COUNTER

OPENSA 3 COUNTER

END LEVEL 3 MULTIPLE COUNTERS

OPENSA-DEPENSA

LEVEL 1 BLOCKING | Depensa 7

The feeder attacks with *Opensa 7* and the defender executes *Depensa 7* in response. Start in *Preparar* (Fig. 1). Feeder sinks their weight as they raise their weapon above their head (Fig. 2)., then steps forward with their right leg as they execute an Opensa 7 downward attack to the crown of the defender's head, and in response the defender raises their weapon to protect their head as they offline to the left (Fig. 3). As the feeder brings their weapon down, the defender meets the weapon with their own, while simultaneously reaching for the opponent's weapon hand with their alive hand (Fig. 4); and as they shift their weight into a left-leaning forward stance, knocks the opponent's weapon to the side and captures the opponent's weapon hand with their *Ngangáng Buáya* (Fig. 5).

LEVEL 2 COUNTER | Depensa 7 > Opensa 1

The defence against *Opensa 7* (Fig. 1-5) described above, is followed up by the defender applying a *pigar* to the opponent's weapon hand, pushing it away and down, as they swing their weapon out to the right (Fig. 6), and raising their weapon (Fig. 7), executes an *Opensa 1* downward diagonal forehand counter (Fig. 8), terminating in a *Serrada* position (Fig. 9).

LEVEL 3 MULTIPLE COUNTERS | Depensa 7 > Opensa 1, 2, 3

The defence against *Opensa 7* (Fig. 1-5) described above, is followed up the *Opensa 1* counter (Fig. 6-9). Then the defender raises their weapon above their left shoulder (Fig. 10), as they execute an *Opensa 2* downward diagonal backhand counter (Fig. 11), as they shift their weight into a right-leaning forward stance (Fig. 12). With their weapon now in a low *Abierta* position, they step to the left (Fig. 13), and as they shift their weight onto their left foot, execute an *Opensa 3* upward forehand counter to the feeder's lead leg (Fig. 14), terminating in a left-leaning forward stance with the weapon in a *Serrada* position (Fig. 15).

ALL LEVELS START HERE

END LEVEL 1 BLOCKING

TRANSITION

OPENSA 1 COUNTER
END LEVEL 2 COUNTER

OPENSA 3 COUNTER

END LEVEL 3 MULTIPLE COUNTERS

OPENSA-DEPENSA

⬤ 8

LEVEL 1 BLOCKING | Depensa 8

The feeder attacks with *Opensa 8* and the defender executes *Depensa 8* in response. Start in *Preparar* (Fig. 1). Feeder starts to step forward with their right leg as they drop the point of their weapon (Fig. 2), while the defender starts to lift their weapon and swing their lead leg to the rear (Fig. 3). As the feeder completes their step, and starts to *Totsada* (thrust) towards the defender's torso, the defender executes a *Waslik* defence knocking their opponent's weapon to the side (Fig. 4), and reaching out with their *Ngangáng Buáya* (crocodile mouth) towards the opponent's weapon hand (Fig. 5).

LEVEL 2 COUNTER | Depensa 8 > Opensa 3

The defence against *Opensa 8* (Fig. 1-5) described above, is followed up by *Pigar* to the opponent's weapon hand, pushing it upwards and inwards (Fig. 6), as the defender flips or circles their hand into a *Kayâ* (palm up) position (Fig. 7); and then steps forward with their right leg (Fig. 8), executing an *Opensa 3* upward diagonal counter to the opponent's lead leg (Fig. 9), completing their action in a *Serrada* position.

LEVEL 3 MULTIPLE COUNTERS | Depensa 4 > Opensa 3, 9, 10

The defence against *Opensa 8* (Fig. 1-5) described above, is followed up with the *Opensa 3* counter (Fig. 6-9). Flipping into a *Kulob* (palm down) position, and with weapon raised in a high *Serrada* position over their left shoulder, the defender begins turning to the right (Fig. 10), as they step to the side of their opponent with their left leg, executing an *Opensa 9* horizontal counter to the side of the opponent's head, and applying a *Pigar* to the opponent's weapon arm to prevent a counterattack (Fig. 11 & 12). Maintaining the *Pigar*, the defender raises their weapon above their head as if applying a *Payong* (umbrella block), while stepping to the right with their right leg (Fig. 13), and pivoting on their right leg, executes an *Opensa 10* horizontal counter to the opponent's neck (Fig. 14), stepping back with their left foot to form a forward stance, as they complete the counter (Fig. 15).

BERNAS ESTOCADAS

ALL LEVELS START HERE

END LEVEL 1 BLOCKING

TRANSITION

OPENSA 3 COUNTER

END LEVEL 2 COUNTER

OPENSA 9 COUNTER

OPENSA 10 COUNTER

END LEVEL 3 MULTIPLE COUNTERS

OPENSA-DEPENSA

LEVEL 1 BLOCKING | Depensa 9

The feeder attacks with *Opensa 9* and the defender executes *Depensa 9* in response. Start in *Preparar* (Fig. 1). Feeder starts to bring their left foot forward as they chamber their weapon over their left shoulder as they start to swing their left hand forward (Fig. 2)., while the defender begins stepping forward to meet the attack (Fig. 3). As the feeder executes their Opensa 9 horizontal Waslik attack to the defender's head, the defender meets the opponent's weapon with their *Payong* (umbrella block) while simultaneously parrying the opponent's hand to the side (Fig. 4). The defender then terminates their counter finishing in a low *Abierta* position while maintaining their *Pigar* on the opponent's weapon hand (Fig. 5).

LEVEL 2 COUNTER | Depensa 9 > Opensa 1

The defence against *Opensa 9* (Fig. 1-5) described above, is followed up by flipping the defender flipping their wrist into a Kayâ (palm up) position (Fig. 6), then applying their *Pigar* to push the opponent's weapon hand away and down, raising their weapon out to the right side (Fig. 7), executing an *Opensa 1* (Fig. 8), and finishing in a low *Abierta* position (Fig. 9).

LEVEL 3 MULTIPLE COUNTERS | Depensa 9 > Opensa 1, 2, 3

The defence against *Opensa 9* (Fig. 1-5) described above, is followed up with the *Opensa 1* counter (Fig. 6-9). Then the defender raises their weapon above their left shoulder (Fig. 10), and executes an *Opensa 2* downward diagonal backhand counter (Fig. 11), as they shift their weight into a right-leaning forward stance (Fig. 12). With their weapon now in a low *Abierta* position, they step to the left (Fig. 13), and as they shift their weight onto their left foot, execute an *Opensa 3* counter towards the feeder's lead-leg with an upward forehand attack (Fig. 14), terminating in a left-leaning forward stance with the weapon in an *Serrada* position (Fig. 15).

ALL LEVELS START HERE

END LEVEL 1 BLOCKING

TRANSITION

OPENSA 1 COUNTER — **END LEVEL 2 COUNTER**

OPENSA 2 COUNTER

OPENSA 3 COUNTER — END LEVEL 3 MULTIPLE COUNTERS

OPENSA-DEPENSA

LEVEL 1 BLOCKING | Depensa 10

The feeder attacks with *Opensa 10* and the defender executes *Depensa 10* in response. Start in *Preparar* (Fig. 1). Feeder steps forward with their right leg as they start to bring their weapon up to their right shoulder in a high *Abierta* position (Fig. 2). As they begin shiting their weight onto their lead right leg the defender begins stepping forward to meet the attack with their weapon slightly raised (Fig. 3). As the feeder completes their *Labô* horizontal *Opensa 10* attack to the side of the defender's head, the defender meets the attack with their own weapon held vertically, and their *Ngangáng Buáya* (crocodile mouth)capturing the opponent's weapon hand (Fig. 4).

KÁMBIO | Switching sides

The defence against *Opensa 10* (Fig. 1-4) described above, is followed up a technique called *Kámbio* (swapping or switching gears) in which the defender raises their *Punyo* while maintaining weapon contact (Fig. 5), and presses their forearm against the opponent's forearm as they push it to the side (Fig. 6), applying a *Pigar* to the opponent's weapon arm to complete the switch from the inside to the outside position as they raise their weapon over their right shoulder (Fig. 7).

LEVEL 2 COUNTER | Depensa 10 > Kámbio > Opensa 1

Having completed their defence against *Opensa 10* (Fig. 1-4) described above, and executed the follow up *Kámbio* to switch from the inside to the outside (Fig. 5-7), the defender then continues to push the opponent's arm away with their *Pigar*, as they commence an *Opensa 1* counter from the high *Abierta* position they are in (Fig. 8), attacking the opponent's head with their *Tapás* downward diagonal forehand counter (Fig. 9), as they stand tall and shift their weight to the left (Fig. 10).

LEVEL 3 MULTIPLE COUNTERS | Depensa 10 > Kámbio > Opensa 1, 2, 3, 4

The defence against *Opensa 10* (Fig. 1-4) described previously, followed by the *Kámbio* to switch sides from the inside to the outside (Fig. 5-7), flows into an *Opensa 1* counter (Fig. 8-10). Then from the low Serrada position (Fig. 11), the defender raises their weapon above the level of their left shoulder into a high *Serrada* position (Fig. 12), and executes an *Opensa 2* downward diagonal backhand *Tapás* counter (Fig. 13), as they shift their weight onto their right leg and follow their *Tapás* with their alive hand (Fig. 14), completing the action in a right-leaning forward stance while checking the opponent's weapon arm with a *Pigar* (Fig. 15). Pushing the opponent's arm away to clear space and rotating their weapon hand from a *Kulob* (palm down) to *Kayâ* (palm up) position (Fig. 16), the defender commences their *Hágbas* upward diagonal forehand *Opensa 3* counter to the opponent's lead leg (Fig. 17), as they shift their weight onto their left foot, finishing the counter in a high *Serrada* position with their weapon hand in a *Kayâ* (palm up) position (Fig. 18). Then as they rotate their weapon so that their hand is now in a Kulob (palm down) position, they sink their weight and swing their weapon in a circular arc as they step right (Fig. 19), executing their *Hágbas* upward diagonal backhand *Opensa 4* counter to the opponent's lead leg as they shift their weight to the right (Fig. 20), terminating in a low right-leaning forward stance with the weapon in an *Abierta* position as they reach out to check the opponent's weapon arm with a *Pigar* (Fig. 21).

ALL LEVELS START HERE

END LEVEL 1 BLOCKING

TRANSITION WITH KAMBIO

END TRANSITION

OPENSA 1 COUNTER

OPENSA 4 COUNTER

END LEVEL 3 MULTIPLE COUNTERS

OPENSA-DEPENSA

LEVEL 1 BLOCKING | Depensa 11

The feeder attacks with *Opensa 11* and the defender executes *Depensa 11* in response. Start in *Preparar* (Fig. 1). Feeder shifts their weight onto their right leg as they shift their weapon off the centreline into a *Serrada* position (Fig. 2)., and as they start to push off with their left foot the feeder begins to swing their weapon as if to *Hágbas* (cut the grass) with a backhand attack, while the defender draws their weapon downward and forward in a half circle (Fig. 3). As the feeder begins cross-stepping their left leg behind their right and attacks upward at the defender's groin, the defender reaches towards the opponent's weapon hand with their alive hand (Fig. 4). As the feeder completes their cross-step and *Opensa 11* attack, the defender applies their *Ngangáng Buáya* to the opponet's weapon hand and meets the weapon with their *Depensa 11* block (Fig. 5).

LEVEL 2 COUNTER | Depensa 11 > Opensa 2

The defence against *Opensa 11* (Fig. 1-5) described above, is followed up by *Pigar* to the opponent's weapon hand, pushing it downward and to the side (Fig. 6), allowing the defender to raise their weapon beside their left shoulder as they shift their weight to the right (Fig. 7), making space for the execution of a *Opensa 2* downward diagonal backhand *Tapás* counter (Fig. 8), terminating in a low *Abierta* position (Fig. 9).

LEVEL 3 MULTIPLE COUNTERS | Depensa 11 > Opensa 2, 3, 4, 3

The defence against *Opensa 11* (Fig. 1-5) described above, is followed up with the *Opensa 2* counter (Fig. 6-9). Then the defender rotates their wrist into a *Kayâ* (supine) position (Fig. 10), and executes a high *Opensa 3* counter to the opponent's arm as they start to shift their weight to the left (Fig. 11), completing their counter in a left-leaning forward stance, weapon held in a high *Serrada* position (Fig. 12). Then rotating their wrist into a *Kulob* (prone) position, the defender steps to the right (Fig. 13), executing a *Hagbás* (grass-cutting) *Opensa 4* counter targeting the legs (Fig. 14), checking the opponent's weapon hand with their *Pigar* as they complete the counter in a right-leaning forward stance (Fig. 15). Then rotating their wrist once more into Kayâ (Fig. 16), the defender shifts their weight to the left as the execute their *Opensa 3* (Fig. 17 & 18).

OPENSA-DEPENSA

ALL LEVELS START HERE

BERNAS ESTOCADAS

END LEVEL 1 BLOCKING

TRANSITION

OPENSA 2 COUNTER

END LEVEL 2 COUNTER

OPENSA 4 COUNTER

OPENSA 3 COUNTER

END LEVEL 3 MULTIPLE COUNTERS

OPENSA-DEPENSA

12

LEVEL 1 BLOCKING | Depensa 12

The feeder attacks with *Opensa 12* and the defender executes *Depensa 12* in response. Start in *Preparar* (Fig. 1). Feeder sinks their weight as the draw their weapon in towards their torso, the point aimed at the opponent, and their alive hand brought up to guard their neck area (Fig. 2). Then as they step forward, the defender starts to step diagonally forward with their left foot, moving to the outside of the attack (Fig. 3), meeting the opponent's *Totsada* (thrust) aimed at their face, with their own weapon, knocking it to the side with a *Waslik* (whipping) motion (Fig. 4), and applying their *Ngangáng Buáya* (crocodile mouth) to the opponent's forearm as they complete their motion in a left-leaning forward stance (Fig. 5).

LEVEL 2 COUNTER | Depensa 12 > Opensa 1

The defence against *Opensa 12* (Fig. 1-5) described above, is followed up by *pigar* to the opponent's weapon hand, pushing it away and down, allowing the defender's weapon to naturally chamber high above their right shoulder (Fig. 6), and making space for the execution of a *Opensa 1* downward diagonal forehand *Tapás* (tree-cutting) counter (Fig. 7), as they shift their weight onto their left foot (Fig. 8), and complete the counter in a low *Serrada* position (Fig. 9).

LEVEL 3 MULTIPLE COUNTERS | Depensa 12 > Opensa 1, 2, 3

The defence against *Opensa 12* (Fig. 1-5) described above, is followed up the *Opensa 1* counter (Fig. 6-9). Then the defender raises their weapon into a *Serrada* position (Fig. 10), as they step and shift their weight to the right while executing an *Opensa 2* downward diagonal backhand *Tapás* (tree-cutting) counter (Fig. 11), completing the counter in a right-leaning forward stance and applying *Pigar* to the opponent's weapon arm to prevent a counterattack (Fig. 12). With their weapon now in a low *Abierta* position, the defender steps to the left (Fig. 13), and as they shift their weight onto their left foot, executes an *Opensa 3* diagonal upward *Hagbás* (grass-cutting) counter towards the opponent's lead leg (Fig. 14), terminating in a low left-leaning forward stance (Fig. 15).

ALL LEVELS START HERE

END LEVEL 1 BLOCKING

TRANSITION

OPENSA 1 COUNTER

END LEVEL 2 COUNTER

OPENSA 2 COUNTER

BERNAS ESTOCADAS

OPENSA 3 COUNTER — END LEVEL 3 MULTIPLE COUNTERS

AFTERWORD

We hope you have enjoyed this book, and that it has achieved its goal of providing a solid introduction to the art of Bernas Estocadas. You will notice that although a great deal of the focus of the first half of the book was on the *Bastón* (stick), that the later half of the book demonstrated the *Opensa-Depensa* with a *Talíbong* (sword). It is certainly the case that the *12 Opensa* and *12 Depensa* covered in this volume are the heart of the system, and have their application with other weapons, such as the *Doble Bastón* (double sticks), *Espada y Daga* (sword & dagger), *Dága* (knife), *Olisi* (walking stick), and *Súngkod* (longstick or staff). There are also unarmed applications taught through the Estokido system. What should be obvious by now is the extent to which the Bernas Estocadas system is geared for handling multiple opponents. This will have been particularly evident in the chapter on the *Dágway* (forms), but may also have been revealed in the *Palakát* (footwork drills) that were covered right at the start of the book, where we demonstrated striking and blocking while moving to and fro, advancing and retreating. We certainly hope you are keen to see more of the Bernas Estocadas system, and we look forward to providing you with additional volumes that extend your knowledge, skill, and understanding.

GLOSSARY

The Bernas Estocadas system is from the Negros Occidental region of the Philippines. Thus, the majority of terms are from the Ilonggo language. Spelling of Filipino martial arts terms is a fraught space, as vowel sounds like 'o' can be represented by 'u' and vice versa; or 'i' may be replaced by 'y'; and when writing Spanish loan words, some authors will use the Spanish 'c' while others use the Filipino 'k'. To try to eliminate some confusion, the spellings used in this glossary come from the online *hiligaynon.pinoydictionary.com,* and the accents placed upon the words, which are often written without them, are used here to help non-Ilonggo speakers understand where the stress is placed for better pronunciation.

ABANÍKO (v.), to fan; to strike with a fanning motion. In Bernas Estocadas one of the advanced PALABÚLAK strikes.

ABESEDARIO (n.), ABCs, basics, or fundamentals.

ABIERTA (n.), open; an open guard position; the opposite of SERRADA.

ALKONTRA KARGADA (v.), (from KONTRA "versus" and KARGADA "cargo or load"), the principle of "meeting the force" when engaged in defence. The opposite of PAÁNOD.

ANTÍNG-ANTÍNG (n.), amulets, talismens, or charms that are believed by the wearer to give them special powers, such as an ability to avoid being cut. Sometimes warn as tattoos.

ANTIS (pr.), before; to anticipate the opponent's intent, and to initiate your counter as they prepare to attack, before they have a chance to move. (See also ORAMISMO and TAPOS).

BAKÂ (v.), to straddle; in Bernas Estocadas the Horse Stance.

BASTÓN (n.), stick or cane; in Bernas Estocadas a stick of 29 inches. Also one of the names given to the practice of stick-fighting in GM Bernas' youth.

BASTÓNERO (n.), a stick-fighter (a term that suggests a lack of refined skill or formal training). (See as an alternative, ESKRIMADOR).

BÓLO (n.), a large knife, machete or short sword, common as a "working blade" or utility weapon in the Philippines, and famously used by Filipinos in WWII.

DAGASÓ (n.), literally "dagger smoke"; in Ilonggo the term used for the art of knife fighting.

DAGDAG (v.), drop; to strike straight downwards.

DÁGWAY (n.), form; in Bernas Estocadas forms start out as a pre-set routine, but ultimately provide a structured base for improvisation.

DE LÁSTIKO (n.), elastic; an elastic strike that snaps out and back along the same trajectory.

DE PONDO (v.), to put, park, or anchor; a strike that definitively stops at its intended target.

DEPENSA (v.), defence; in Bernas Estocadas the defensive techniques, and applied specifically to the 12 Blocks.

DERECHO (n.), direct; a direct strike that penetrates through the target.

EKIS (n.), a letter X; in Bernas Estocadas the Cross Stance.

ESKRIMADOR (n.), a person with well developed skill in the combative use of the stick and sword. (See as an alternative, BASTÓNERO).

ESPÁDA Y DÁGA (n.), the sword and dagger method of fighting.

GARÁHE (n., v.), garage; to park or chamber your stick in a resting position on your arm or shoulder.

GINÚNTING (n.), a sword, generally with a straight cutting edge, and a curved spine. (See also TALIBÓNG).

GÚNTING (n., v.), scissors or to scissor; using a crossing motion to intercept the opponent's weapon arm, simultaneously parrying and hitting or cutting.

HÁGBAS (v.), to cut the grass; an upward strike to the knees or elbows.

HÁNAS (v.), to drill, train, rehearse, or habituate. In Bernas Estocadas, used to describe controlled sparring pressure-testing exercises.

HILÁY LIKÓD (n.), lean to the rear; in Bernas Estocadas the Back Stance.

HILÁY TUBANG (n.), lean to the front; in Bernas Estocadas the Forward Stance.

ÍMO-ÁKON (n.), yours-mine; the turn-taking 'give-and-take' drill in Bernas Estocadas; the equivalent of SOMBRADA in other systems.

KAGÁT (v.), to snap, seize, or bite; the technique of closing the NGANGÁNG BUÁYA (crocodile's mouth) around the opponent's hand or wrist.

KÁMBIO or KÁMBIADA (v.), to swap or switch gears; a technique for switching sides of your opponent's arm through forearm or weapon contact.

KARENZA (v.) most likely from the Cebuano word KARANSA meaning "to be active, move about, or dance about"; in FMA circles it means improvised freeform shadowboxing or shadow-fencing.

KAYÂ (n.), supine; an open wrist, or palm facing up position of the hand. The opposite of KULOB. In Cebuano systems this position is called HAYANG.

KÍWAL (v.), to lever; using your arm, leg, or torso to add leverage to a strike.

KINAÁDMAN (n.), "old knowledge" or learning, wisdom, cleverness. The name often given to the knowledge of stick fighting in Escalante during GM Bernas' youth.

KULOB (n.), prone; a closed wrist, or palm facing down position of the hand. The opposite of KAYÂ.

LAB-ÁNAY (v.), "slash first"; a blade versus blade drill.

LABÔ (v.), to strike or slash; a horizontal forehand strike to the opponent's head (ie. Opensa 10).

LAKÓT (v.), to mix; in Bernas Estocadas, an advanced drill in which the strikes that start in ABIERTA are combined with strikes that start in SERRADA, and vice versa.

LARGO MANO (n.), Long Hand; in Filipino Martial Arts this is the range at which you can hit the opponent's hand with the tip of your stick, and a style of fighting in which you use your reach to fight at the maximum distance you can, aiming to 'defang the snake' or strike the opponent's weapon hand, before moving in to finish.

MANUNÚDLÒ (n.), Instructor; the teaching rank in Bernas Estocadas.

NGANGÁNG BUÁYA (n.), open mouth of the crocodile; the position of the alive hand so it is ready to grasp the opponent's hand (see also KAGÁT to snap, seize, or bite).

OLISI (n.), a rod or stick; in Bernas Estocadas a stick of 36 inches, usually with a protuberance at one end that is used like the pommel of a sword, to stoop one loosing one's grip on the weapon.

OPENSA (n., v.), offence or attack; the offensive striking techniques of Bernas Estocadas, applied specifically to the 12 Strikes.

OPENSA-DEPENSA (n., v.), attack-defence; the fundamental partner drill in Bernas Estocadas in which the defender executes the 12 Depensa, in response to the 12 Opensa delivered by the feeder.

ORAMISMO (pr.), at the same time; to counter the opponent in the same timing as their attack. (See also ANTIS and TAPOS).

ORASYÓN (n.), a prayer or oration to the Divine, saints, or spirits; in Filipino Martial Arts often a special and secret incantation used as a means of empowering an amulet (see ANTÍNG-ANTÍNG).

PAÁNOD (v.), to float down the river; in Bernas Estocadas, the term used to describe "going with the force" of an attack, in contrast to ALKONTRA KARGADA.

PAGSOLÓNDAN (n.), rules; the fundamental principles to be followed.

PAHÚWAY (v.), to rest; a natural standing position with one's weapon hanging by their side.

PALABÚLAK (n.), flowering; the advanced strikes of Bernas Estocadas including: ABANÍKO, PÁLPAL, WASIWAS, and REDONDA.

PALAKÁT (v.), to go; footwork.

PALÁPAW (v.), to pass; in Bernas Estocadas a passing drill.

PÁLPAL (v.), to stake or peg; one of the four PALABÚLAK of Bernas Estocadas in which you strike downwards with the the side of your weapon.

PANG-ÁGAW (v.), to take or snatch; the term for weapon disarming.

PANG-ÁWAY (v.), fighting; in Bernas Estocadas, the advanced combative drills of the system.

PANGÚYAT (v.), to grasp hold; the method of holding the weapon.

PANÍNDOG (n.), to stand; the stances in Bernas Estocadas.

PÁRES PÁRES (v.), to couple or to pair; a fundamental drill in Bernas Estocadas in which the 12 strikes and 12 blocks are practiced in pairs.

PASUNÓD (v.), to follow; in Bernas Estocadas, practicing strikes or blocks in a consecutive numerical sequence.

PÁYONG (n.), umbrella; a block in which the tip of one's weapon is pointing to the ground and the weapon is used as a shield.

PEKITI TIRSIA (n.), Literally "Close Third" (the equivalent of CORTO MANO, one of the three ranges of weapon combat widely referred to as Largo, Medio, and Corto, in contemporary Filipino Martial Arts and referring to the range in which you can strike the opponent with the butt of your weapon, or both hands); Probably best translated into English as "Close Quarters" and used in Ilonggo as a reference to Eskrima in general, especially those systems of Eskrima with an emphasis on in-fighting.

PIGAR (n.), to push and apply pressure to the opponent's weapon arm in order to maintain control or clear the line for a clean counterstrike.

PÍNÙTI (n.), a cutlass type sword or Bólo, that is relatively straight, with a slightly curved belly, and either a clip point or drop point tip.

POSISYÓN (n., v.), to position; methods of positioning your stick for combat. (See also SERRADA, ABIERTA, and SÉNTRO).

PREPARAR (v.), to prepare; the system's central on-guard position.

PÚNGKÒ (v.), to sit or be seated; in Bernas Estocadas the Cat Stance.

REDONDA (n.), round; a circular strike that starts and ends in the same location, that forms one of the four PALABÚLAK of Bernas Estocadas.

SAGÁNG (v.), to stop, prevent, ward off, or parry; blocking techniques.

SAGÁNG-SAGÁNG (v.), the name given to friendly "light-sparring", sometimes used as a warm up to something more intense.

SALUDO (n., v.), to salute; a sign of respect and gratitude, by bringing the weapon hand over the heart, and bowing.

SÉNTRO (n.), central; a guard position in which you place your weapon on the centreline.

SERRADA (n.), closed; a closed guard position in which one's weapon crosses the centreline; the opposite of ABIERTA.

SÚNGKOD (n.), a short staff or walking stick; in Bernas Estocadas a long-stick of 45 inches.

TAGDUHÁ (v.), in couples or twos; a drill in which the 12 strikes are combined in two-strike combinations.

TAGTÁTLO (v.), in triplets or threes; a drill in which the 12 strikes are combined in three-strike combinations.

TALIBÓNG (n.), a large bolo, or sword, typically with a straight back and curved belly. (See also GINÚNTING).

TAPÁS (v.), to cut down; the downward diagonal strikes of Bernas Estocadas (ie. Opensa 1 & 2).

TAPÍ (v.), to brush off, or knock off course with a sudden blow; in Bernas Estocadas a parrying manoeuvre with the alive hand.

TAPOS (pr.), after; to allow the opponent's attack to conclude before executing your own counterattack (ie. evading and then countering). (See also ANTIS and ORAMISMO).

TIÉMPO or TYEMPO (n.), time or timing. (See also ANTIS, ORAMISMO, and TAPOS).

TOTSADA (v.), to thrust; the thrusting attacks of Bernas Estocadas (Opensa 5, 6, 8, & 12) that together form a cross shape.

TÚMBADA (v.), to drop or knockdown; striking the ground with one's weapon to power your strike and evade an opponent's attack or counter.

WASIWAS (v.), to wave to and fro, to brandish, or to wag; the back and forth horizontal strikes that form one of the four PALABÚLAK of the system.

WÁSLIK (v.), to strike backwards, to whip, or turn back; the key blocking action against attacks on the centreline in Bernas Estocadas (ie. Depensa 7, 8 & 12)

WEDO (n., v.), (from the Spanish OIDO meaning "hearing") to learn by ear, or learning without formal instruction; a kind of street smarts; the old informal way of teaching Filipino Martial Arts.

WITIK (v.), to flip or flick; in Bernas Estocadas an upward vertical striking action (ie. Opensa 11).

BERNAS ESTOCADAS
Abesedario Curriculum Overview

This diagram shows the relationship of the various aspects of the Bernas Estocadas stick and blade *Abesedario* curriculum covered in this book. Note: this is not a comprehensive representation of the entire system.

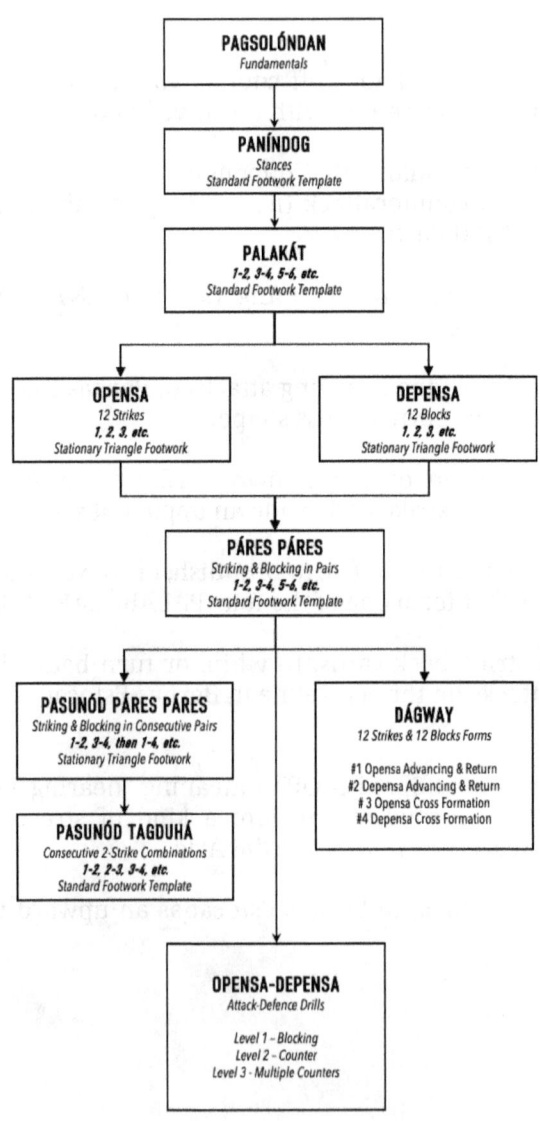

Grandmaster
WILLIAM BERNAS

Grandmaster William Bernas is a proud Negrosanon, who was born in the city of Escalante in the Negros Occidental region of the Philippines. He originally studied to be a graphic artist, before later becoming a massage therapist and full-time martial arts instructor. He commenced his martial art training at a young age, learning in the traditional *Wedo* style of instruction, under the informal tutelage of his Grandfather and Uncle. He has engaged in serious study of Karate, Aikido, Praying Mantis Kung-Fu, and Tai Chi, in addition to the Filipino Martial Arts. In the 1980s he studied within the Navales Arnis Clinic of Grandmaster Hortencio Navales, under the direct tutelage of Grandmaster Romeo Postrano, with whom he became a close "kumpadre". He credits his time as an Instructor and student within the Navales Arnis Clinic as bringing a systematic approach to his thinking about Filipino Martial Arts instruction, which led him to develop his own system, which he calls Bernas Estocadas (or the Bernas way of fighting). When not teaching martial arts at his local university, online, or in a park, or preparing healthy meals from freshly picked ingredients growing wild in his neighbourhood, you will find this sexagenarian lifting weights at the local gym.

Manunudlo
PAOLO PAGALING

Manunudlo Paolo Pagaling is the international training director for both De Campo 1-2-3 Original and Bernas Estocadas, with instructor credentials in De Campo 1-2-3 Original, Bernas Estocadas, Estokada De Campo, and Baraw Sugbo (Arnes Diablo). He is also the developer of Praktikali, a system that takes an analytical approach to understanding the Filipino Martial Arts. Paolo commenced his study of martial arts in his youth, in the Korean martial art of Hwarang-Do, and a number of Filipino Martial Arts that he would later come to realise had been influenced by the De Campo 1-2-3 Original system developed by Professor Jose Caballero in 1925. Having studied a number of its variants, Paolo sought out to study the original De Campo system with its reigning heir, Master Jomalin Caballero, becoming its first Maestro in the current generation. Committed to preserving the traditional Filipino Martial Arts he has studied, Paolo has worked with Master Jomalin Caballero (De Campo 1-2-3 Original), Grandmaster Eduardo Ceniza (Arnes Diablo/Baraw Sugbo), and Grandmaster William Bernas (Bernas Estocadas) to preserve their systems in the form of video recordings that have been curated into highly respected online courses. Through the vehicle of online teaching, Paolo is today training students all around the world.

Manunudlo
ROBERT J. PARKES

Manunudlo Robert Parkes is an Associate Professor in the School of Education at the University of Newcastle, Australia; Founder and Executive Editor of the successful academic journal *Historical Encounters;* and Chief Instructor of the Kali Newcastle Filipino Martial Arts Academy. He has instructor credentials in Chinese, Japanese, and Filipino Martial Arts. He began martial arts training in Wing Chun Kung-Fu in 1980, and his earliest exposures to Filipino Martial Arts were in seminars with Guro Dan Inosanto in 1982, and through Modern Arnis in the mid-1990s. In 2019 he travelled to the Philippines, with his daughter, Rebekah Parkes, to study De Campo 1-2-3 Original with Maestro Paolo Pagaling, who later introduced him to Grandmaster William Bernas. He has been training under both gentlemen since that time, and holds instructor ranks in both De Campo 1-2-3 Original and Bernas Estocadas. In 2021, inspired by Paolo's efforts to preserve rare FMA systems like De Campo and Bernas Estocadas on video, and combining his academic and personal interests, Robert initiated his Eskrima Media publishing project, in which he hopes to curate and produce a series of volumes (of which this is the first) promoting and documenting these intangible forms of Filipino cultural heritage in book form.

www.ingramcontent.com/pod-product-compliance
Lightning Source LLC
Chambersburg PA
CBHW050857160426
43194CB00011B/2186